CREATING A
CULTURE OF GRACE
IN A CLIMATE OF SHAME

BY NICK STUMBO

SAFE

© Copyright Nick Stumbo
Printed in the United States of America
ALL RIGHTS RESERVED
www.puredesire.org

Published by
Pure Desire Ministries International
www.puredesire.org | Gresham, Oregon | November 2017

ISBN 978-1-943291-85-4

No part of this publication may be reproduced, stored in a retrieval system, or transmitted in any form by any means—electronic, mechanical, photocopying, recording or otherwise—without prior written consent of Pure Desire Ministries International, except as provided by the United States of America copyright law.

Unless otherwise indicated, all Scripture quotations are taken from the Holy Bible, New Living Translation, copyright © 1996, 2004, 2007, 2013, 2015 by Tyndale House Foundation. Used by permission of Tyndale House Publishers, Inc., Carol Stream, Illinois 60188. All rights reserved.

Scripture quotations marked (NKJV) taken from the New King James Version®. Copyright © 1982 by Thomas Nelson. Used by permission. All rights reserved.

Scripture quotations marked (NIV) are taken from the Holy Bible, New International Version®, NIV®. Copyright © 1973, 1978, 1984, 2011 by Biblica, Inc.™ Used by permission of Zondervan. All rights reserved worldwide. www.zondervan.com. The "NIV" and "New International Version" are trademarks registered in the United States Patent and Trademark Office by Biblica, Inc.™

CONTENTS

FOREWORD ········ 7

ACKNOWLEDGMENTS ········ 11

INTRODUCTION ········ 13

1. WHERE DID WE GO WRONG? ········ 23

2. I SEE YOU ········ 35

3. THE WORST BEST DAY ········ 55

4. COVER ME ········ 81

5. PEOPLE OF GRACE ········ 105

6. DO UNTO OTHERS ········ 131

7. THE GRACE OF CALLING ········ 159

8. STAYING SAFE ········ 181

❝ Whether you are a pastor, church leader, parent or the average person in church Sunday morning, this book is for you. Today, like never before, the church is full of wounded and broken people; those who recognize the corrosive nature of hopelessness and who struggle to create community in their church body. Through remarkable stories and biblical truths, Nick Stumbo provides the practical application steps necessary to revive the body of Christ—rejuvenate the lives of men and women, rebuild relationships, and restore families. I'm excited to see how God will use *Safe: Creating a Culture of Grace in a Climate of Shame* to invigorate His church.

JOSH McDOWELL
AUTHOR AND SPEAKER

❝ As a psychologist, I have worked with thousands of couples over the years. And, even in a "good" marriage, I've seen too many settle for false intimacy, as they hide the worst of who they are from one another. There's a better way, and Nick Stumbo shows us how. In this candid book, Nick reveals a pathway for true change. If you're looking to take your relationship to a deeper level, read this book. Don't let shame keep you in bondage and isolation. Discover grace and safety in your relationships like never before.

LES PARROTT, PhD
#1 NEW YORK TIMES BESTSELLING
AUTHOR OF CRAZY GOOD SEX

FOREWORD
BY DR. TED ROBERTS

In 2010, as I spoke at an annual pastor's conference, I had no idea what God was about to put into motion—a sequence of events that not only changed Nick Stumbo's life, but had a profound impact on my life and ministry.

As a pastor, sexual addiction professional, and founder of Pure Desire Ministries International, I have spent the past 30 years counseling men who struggle with pornography and sexually addictive behaviors. I have spoken at conferences around the world and this conference wasn't much different. Three hundred plus pastors, and some of their wives, were in the audience.

When it comes to sexual addiction, my approach always includes scientific and statistical data, poured over a foundation of biblical truth. Typically, I start off by helping the audience understand how the human brain works and how their brain becomes sexually addicted. I include other factors that influence addictive behaviors, such as affect regulation, attachment, child development, and trauma. My intent is never to put the blame on parents or others who may have unknowingly contributed to our personal trauma. But this truth remains: we cannot break free from sexual bondage without God's grace and without processing our past trauma. We have to heal the wounds of our soul from the inside out.

While I have dedicated my life to helping pastors who struggle with pornography and sexual addiction, this is a tough crowd. To broach this subject in any arena is challenging; but, to intentionally present the message of sexual bondage to a group of men who are the pillars of godliness in their church—who live and model integrity, and obviously love God with all their heart—is not easy. One of the greatest weapons the enemy uses against us is denial: denial that we have an issue that is out of control and slowing eroding our relationship with God and others. Another is shame. Shame buries us under its weight, holding us hostage through fear and isolation. Fear that someone will discover our secret: that we frequent pornography sites, that we seek out inappropriate relationships with coworkers, that we visit strip clubs and prostitutes. Whatever it is that fuels our fear of discovery also propels us into isolation. As we live in isolation, we deceive ourselves into believing that isolation will camouflage the truth—that we are wounded and in need of a lifelong healing that only our Heavenly Father can provide.

At the 2010 conference, I was promoting a partnership program with Pure Desire—a program that allows pastors who struggle with pornography and sexual addiction to receive marriage counseling services at a discounted rate. Furthermore, if a pastor's sexually addictive behaviors met a certain criteria, they could stay in their position of leadership in their church, fully supported by the elder board, while completing the program. Out of the 300 plus pastors who attended the conference, only one pastor came forward: Nick Stumbo.

FOREWORD

Over the next year, my wife, Diane, and I counseled Nick and his wife, Michelle. I have found that many men who struggle with pornography and sexual addiction have a deep father wound, a woundedness that is often unknown to the individual. I cannot tell you how many men I have worked with who outright reject this "father wound" theory, only to recognize—several months later—that the basis of their addictive behavior is due to this level of woundedness.

Following his healing journey, Nick stayed connected with Pure Desire. He and Michelle started groups in their church for men and women who struggle with sexual addiction and betrayal. In 2013, he wrote his personal story in a book, *Setting Us Free*, published by Pure Desire.

When I previously spoke of how God put His plan in motion back in 2010, I could not have imagined what God was going to do unless I witnessed it with my own eyes. As I have entered my "retirement years," it became apparent that I would need to pass on the leadership and vision of my life's work: Pure Desire Ministries International. As we—my wife and I, the Pure Desire Board of Directors, Executive Team, and staff—began to pray about what this succession plan might look like, it was not long before God's plan and purpose for Pure Desire was clear. Nick Stumbo was the perfect candidate.

In the fall of 2016, Nick stepped into the position of Executive Director at Pure Desire. He had been through the clinical program, was thriving as a result of his healing, and was passionate about helping others find freedom from pornography and sexual addiction. It is obvious what God has laid on Nick's heart: "Bring healing to My Church. Help My children understand My boundless love and grace. Teach them how to live in freedom."

All of us need a safe place to heal. In this book, Nick calls on the church to become a community that is safe, a place where biblical grace becomes part of its actual DNA. He powerfully addresses and contrasts society's cheap definition of grace—which includes tolerance, entitlement, and permissiveness—to the depth of what God's grace offers: unconditional love, acceptance, repentance, and forgiveness.

He shares his own story: how, as a pastor, he was able to overcome his addiction to pornography—not by trying harder, but through vulnerability and reaching out for help. God did an amazing work in Nick's life, marriage and family, but He didn't stop there. God did what only He can do, using Nick's confession from the pulpit to transform his church. It became a place where it was okay to not be okay.

This book addresses the critical necessity of a culture of grace written from a pastor's perspective and personal experience. My prayer is that through this book, you will have the opportunity to transform your church culture and community, watching it change and grow into someplace *Safe: Creating a Culture of Grace in a Climate of Shame*.

Dr. Ted Roberts
Founder, Pure Desire Ministries International

ACKNOWLEDGMENTS

I would like to thank my wife, who has always been the biggest fan and best cheerleader of all my writing projects. Thank you for allowing me to write this book in the "margins" of life: time that could have been spent with you and the kids!

I would like to thank the elders and the good people of East Hills Alliance and The Grove Alliance Church in Kelso, Washington. You all modeled love and forgiveness to us. You were such willing participants in our journey to become a culture of grace!

I would like to thank Sauna Winsor, Bryan Roberts, Heather Kolb, and the whole team at Pure Desire. You made this book a reality, from the idea to the editing to the publishing. Thank you for believing in me and in the need for this book.

Finally, I would like to thank my Savior. Jesus, you continue to show me both my need for grace and your endless supply of it. Thank you for giving me this message to share with others.

INTRODUCTION

I have a confession to make. I don't like auto parts stores. If you happen to work at one, I have no problem with you. My issue is with the industry and the environment it creates. You see, part of this confession is to tell you that I know very little about cars. I like driving them, but when it comes to fixing or maintaining them, I run into trouble. I once added a quart of oil to the transmission fluid pan. On another occasion, in an attempt to save gas by coasting in neutral down a steep hill, I shifted the car into reverse while going 70 mph on the freeway. The engine died; I did not.

So when I walk into the auto parts store, I immediately feel out of place. I am intimidated by row after row of parts and supplies, many of which I can hardly identify, let alone name. Invariably, I find myself walking up and down the aisles looking for my needed part—usually something "intense" like a headlight or a spark plug—when a store associate will find me and casually ask, "Can I help you?"

In this situation, I'm always tempted to protest, "No, I know exactly what I'm doing!" But I figure the vacant expression on my face has already given me away as a complete novice when it comes to cars. I sheepishly tell them what I am looking for, worried that even this simple admission of need will elicit scoffing from someone who's an expert in the field; "A headlight? You seriously came in for just a headlight?"

I have never actually had anyone say this, or treat me this way, but I still worry.

I visit auto parts stores as rarely as possible. I feel strange, as though my appearance is a dead giveaway that I don't belong. No, I find it easier to take my car to the experts and let them deal with all the repairs, even the simple ones. It just feels safer to me.

Maybe you feel this way at the auto parts store as well or maybe you don't. But I am guessing that you can relate to having this feeling somewhere. I am also guessing that this is the way many people in our culture feel about the church. I know I did.

Every weekend, people who feel like novices about religion and spirituality walk into church buildings and feel like they are on foreign ground. Young couples venture out and try a small group for the first time. Older couples, who have grown distant from the church since their children left home, return, not knowing what to expect. Many people in these situations fear being exposed for their insufficient knowledge or questionable behavior, while the experts up front are left to do all the real work. The novices do their best to get what they need and then escape out the door before being cornered, feeling embarrassed, or having their lack of expertise exposed.

Did the church set out to make people feel this way? I doubt it. Could the person coming in the door do more to prepare themselves? Probably. But the point isn't to cast blame on why the church has become a place known for lacking grace. The point is to do something about it. So whether you feel as out of place at church as I do at the auto parts store, or you are one of the experts running the whole show, I want us all to consider how the church can be different; how can we become safe?

When I use the word safe, I don't mean it in terms of physically safe; although physical safety can be part of the equation. Or, when sliding into home plate and the umpire calls "safe" as opposed to "out."

INTRODUCTION

What I mean by safe is primarily an emotional state where we feel peace about being who we are. The kind of place where we can let down our guard, stop playing the game, and quit looking over our shoulder. A safe place is usually less about the place itself, and more about the people who occupy that space.

Perhaps for you, your safe place is home or the home you grew up in. Maybe your safe place was Grandma's house or the home of another relative. Some might say that their safe place is a favorite restaurant, bar, or pub. A safe place is where we are eager to arrive and reluctant to leave. We linger as long as we can to enjoy the feeling that we are known and loved just the way we are. A safe place like this is marked by grace. So how do we create this kind of emotional safe place in our homes, groups, or church community?

DREAM A LITTLE

In 2003, I was flipping through radio stations when a country western song struck my curiosity. Toby Keith had just released the song, "I Love This Bar." In it, he croons about how people from all walks of life and all kinds of backgrounds felt safe at the corner bar. His chorus says,

> I love this bar,
> It's my kind of place.
> Just walk in through the front door,
> Puts a big smile on my face.
> It ain't too far, come as you are.
> Mm, mm, mm, mm, mm, I love this bar.[1]

---

1. Keith, T. & Emerick, S. (2003). I Love This Bar. On *Shock'n Y'all* [CD]. Nashville, TN: DreamWorks Nashville.

You may or may not have an affinity for country western music, or bars for that matter, but don't get hung up on that. Do you notice the message of this song? There's a place where it's okay to not be okay. Where, every day, millions of people saddle up to bars around the world because it is where they feel safe.

What if the church was a place where it was okay to not be okay? What if the church made people feel safe? What if the church was made up of people whose arms opened wide enough to embrace any and all wayward sons and daughters? What if the gathering of the church was a place we absolutely had to be, even when we felt as down and rotten as ever? What if, rather than feeling the need to avoid the church and isolate in our pain and brokenness, we felt compelled to go and be with a group that we knew would help bring us to God? Is this kind of place, this kind of a people, even possible?

When we think of a safe place, the church rarely comes to mind. If it does for you, hold on to that place and fight to keep it safe no matter what it takes—you are enjoying a rare commodity in our world. The equation seems to be that the more people you put together, the greater likelihood that people will posture, pose, and put on an act to be accepted by the group. As soon as this happens, safety is lost in favor of performance and acceptance. Grace gets lost in the shuffle while shame multiplies over our inability to live up to the perceived group standard.

Becoming a safe place will rarely, if ever, happen by accident in a group. It must be created by those who know the way; those who have walked a path of grace and know how to call others down that same road. My hope is that this book will give you some very practical—and at times very personal—steps you can take to become one of those people.

INTRODUCTION

Let's talk, and dream together, about how the church can create a different atmosphere; one that is intentional about culture change.

WHO THIS BOOK IS FOR

Hopefully, on some level, you are asking the question, "Is this book for me?" In the book of Ecclesiastes, we read, "Of making many books there is no end, and much study wearies the body." Never have these words been more true than today! Thousands upon thousands of new books come out each year. You can't even begin to read them all. Your time is too valuable to waste on a book that is not applicable to where you are in life. So, I am writing this book for you if you are:

- a church leader or pastor who wants to see your faith community become a more honest, vulnerable, real, and grace-saturated environment.
- a small group leader who has grown weary of surface-level conversations.
- a parent wrestling with how to make your home a haven of safety and trust for your children or grandchildren.
- a man or woman tired of the status quo and fed up with playing church.
- someone who continually sings about, talks about, and hears about God's love but experiences very little of it personally or from others.
- a person who feels isolated by your sin and destructive behavior, unsure how to face it or talk about it; afraid that if you did, you would be rejected or shut out from community.

So rather than finding real community, you sit, week after week, surrounded by people and still feel utterly alone.

- longing to see the church become a relevant, life-changing force that offers real hope in a time filled with many cheap imitations of grace.
- among those of us who hunger for something more in relationships, faith, and life.

If you find yourself in any of these categories, I believe these pages will encourage, challenge and strengthen you. There is hope, because of grace.

A BIT ABOUT ME

The truth is, at some point in my life, I could find myself in every one of those bullet points just listed. I grew up in and around the church from day one, having been born into a pastor's family. I learned how church-culture worked, and learned how to lead it well. But in 2010, I found myself trapped in a grace-less culture. Why? Honestly, it was my own doing. As is often the case, we want to blame a lack of grace on the environment or people around us. But a lack of grace usually stems from our own inability to be a person of grace.

I lacked grace for others because I had none for myself. I was trapped in a shame-filled addiction to pornography.

On the outside, I had it all: a gorgeous wife, three beautiful children, and a healthy, growing church. But on the inside, I was dying. No matter how hard I tried, no matter how much I prayed and read the Bible, I couldn't seem to shake free from a binge-purge cycle of numbing my mind and soul to images online. And this struggle brought my marriage, and with it my ministry, to the very brink of destruction.

INTRODUCTION

I was trapped in shame and isolation. I didn't know how to experience real grace for myself, and I certainly didn't know how to lead others into an experience of grace in their life. As a leader, I was simply replicating the culture that existed inside my own head. Feeling shameful and condemned, I struggled to offer true grace to others.

But God did an amazing work of healing in my soul. He led me into personal freedom and into a new era in my marriage. I became real in my preaching and leading. As my life transformed, so did the environments around me. My marriage, family, and church have become cultures of grace. Not perfect, mind you—I am still a flawed human being on a journey. Yet, this journey has produced fruit both in and around me. I want to share that journey with you by looking at stories from Scripture that paint a way forward.

MY HOPE FOR YOU

As you read, my hope is that you find yourself beginning a new journey. One of the mistakes we can make with grace is believing that it's a destination. We may think that if we could only practice a few simple principles, we would have a culture of grace. Grace can be a simple concept, but I believe that working these truths into our lives, homes, and places of worship can be a complex and multi-layered adventure. Grace isn't a place at which we arrive; grace is a journey we learn to embrace. Each experience of grace—each new understanding or deeper truth that works its way into our soul—takes us farther along the road.

This isn't a fix-it-in-three-simple-steps kind of book, though it includes many ideas and steps that you can take. I don't have

Five Easy Ways to a Grace Culture. If you were looking for that, you probably could have found a blog and been on your way by now. But instead, you chose to pick up this book. You decided to immerse yourself in ideas and concepts for more than a few minutes; and for that I am honored.

What you will find in this book is the answer to some very significant questions. Does grace mean I accept others and their behavior even when I disagree with what they do or how they live? How has our current post-modern culture settled for a thin version of grace that falls short of what God has in mind? Does grace mean turning a blind eye to everyone or everything that hurts me? And on a very personal level, how do I receive grace over areas of my life where I don't feel I deserve any?

Come with me on a journey of discovering the fullness and richness of grace as God truly gives it. I pray that our travels together will bring you into a rich and beautiful experience of God's grace in every arena of your life—personally, relationally, and in your church.

Becoming a place where it's okay to not to be okay will take some time, and even some trials. But the trip is worth taking. As the path stretches before us, consider an alternative to the Toby Keith song I mentioned earlier. In the words of David Crowder's song, "Come As You Are," we are invited into a journey of becoming safe:

> Come out of sadness, from wherever you've been
> Come broken hearted let rescue begin
> Come find your mercy oh sinner come kneel
> Earth has no sorrow that heaven can't heal
> Earth has no sorrow that heaven can't heal

INTRODUCTION

So lay down your burdens
Lay down your shame
All who are broken
Lift up your face
Oh wanderer come home
You're not too far
So lay down your hurt
Lay down your heart
Come as you are

There's hope for the hopeless and all those who've strayed
Come sit at the table, come taste the grace
There's rest for the weary, rest that endures
Earth has no sorrow that heaven can't cure

So lay down your burdens
Lay down your shame
All who are broken
Lift up your face
Oh wanderer come home
You're not too far
So lay down your hurt
Lay down your heart
Come as you are
Come as you are[2]

---

2. Crowder, D., Glover, B., & Maher, M. (2014). Come As You Are [Recorded by artist]. On *Neon Steeple* [CD]. Brentwood, TN: Sparrow Records. Atlanta, GA: Sixstepsrecords.

CHAPTER 1
WHERE DID WE GO WRONG?

I grew up in the great state of Montana. During my teenage years, a regular part of the summer was taking week-long backpacking trips into the rugged and beautiful Rocky Mountains. My father was a pastor and he would organize these trips for a local Christian camp. He was passionate about getting kids into the wilderness, where they could experience God in a new and powerful way. He was good at what he did, and I benefited by watching and growing under his leadership.

After being a "camper" on these trips for many years, as a college student, my father invited me to help as a leader. I was to be the co-director for the camp, and I was eager to stretch my wings and give it a try. On this particular trip, he would be delayed; he went to pick up my younger brother, Andy, who was returning from a mission-trip to Mexico just in time to join us in the mountains. The plan was that I would lead the campers to our first tent site, start getting everyone organized, and then he would show up just an hour or two behind us.

The day went according to plan. We had a trail boss that knew the terrain and he successfully guided us into a picturesque valley where we would spend the first night. I divided the 30 or so teens into tent groups and had them begin setting up. Having quickly set up my own tent, I sat back and watched the other groups work. I was confident that my dad would arrive soon, so I decided to wait before doing anything more. And wait. And wait.

The afternoon became evening, so we started the fires and cooked our meal. We ate, washed up, cleaned dishes, put the food away and still no Dad. The trail boss and I began to exchange questions about what might be delaying their arrival, with worried glances to the sky that was now turning to dusk.

Finally, as darkness began to settle in on our little valley, my dad and brother emerged from the shadowy woods. As they sat around the fire eating their late (and cold) dinner, we heard the story. Dad and Andy had made it to the trailhead as expected and began the hike. About a mile into the trip, they were supposed to take a spur that went off to the left and worked its way toward our valley. "Supposed to" being the key phrase here. Deep in conversation about Andy's trip to Mexico, they had walked right past it.

When they began to look for the spur, they were too late but didn't know it. So they kept on going, continuing to watch for the spur. They found one—the wrong one—but the trail seemed to be headed generally in the right direction, so they took it. Something didn't seem quite right, but they were able to convince themselves they were on track. They trekked several more miles before it became obvious that the trail they were on was not taking them where they wanted to go.

At this point, it was a simple but lengthy process of backtracking down to the main trail, taking the correct spur, and joining us at the campsite. My dad estimated that they had turned a simple 4-mile hike into a grueling 12-mile day. As my dad

CHAPTER 1: WHERE DID WE GO WRONG?

recounted the story that night, I remember him saying something that has stuck with me all these years later. He said, "You know, as we hiked it occurred to me that it didn't matter how fast we walked. It didn't matter how badly we wanted to be here and eat dinner. It didn't matter how sincere our effort was *because we were on the wrong trail*. None of that mattered until we got on the right trail." Leave it to a pastor to turn every misadventure into a great sermon point!

And the point is well made: If you're on the wrong trail, all the effort and desire in the world won't get you to a better place. In fact, you may find yourself farther lost at a faster pace. This can happen all the time with grace. We want to be a culture of grace, but instead, misguided efforts continue to replicate a climate of shame.

JESUS OUR LEADER

From reading the stories in Scripture, one aspect of Jesus' life that becomes abundantly clear is this: *People who were nothing like Jesus liked Jesus.* Everywhere He went, the poor and the outcast flocked to His side. Women and children, who occupied a much lower social rung than Jesus as a Jewish male, were often found in His company. He had a reputation for being a friend of sinners. Gentiles and Samaritans seemed comfortable in His presence. His opponents, the Pharisees, criticized Him because He was always hanging around with tax collectors and sinners. People who were nothing like Jesus liked Jesus!

Could we say the same about ourselves? About the church? In our day, it would seem that people who are nothing like Jesus still like Jesus; they just don't like the church very much. Author Philip Yancey tells this story:

> A prostitute came to me in wretched straits, homeless, sick, unable to buy food for her two-year-old daughter...I asked if she had ever thought of going to a church for help. I will never forget the look of pure, naive shock that crossed her face. "Church!" she cried. "Why would I ever go there? I was already feeling terrible about myself. They'd just make me feel worse."[3]

In Jesus' time, a woman like this would have felt it was safe to run toward Jesus. Now in our time, this woman's refrain echoes the sentiments of many in our society. The body of Christ has become the last place they would turn to find grace.

So how can we change this? The truth is that people who are nothing like Jesus should like the church because we are like Jesus! We have been called to become more like Jesus as we follow Him. If we are more like Him, all kinds of people should like being around us. This is a litmus test of our discipleship.

Does this mean they will always agree with us? No.

Does this mean we will always agree with them or the choices they are making? No.

And neither did Jesus. But He came as a reflection of the Father, and when Jesus looked at people and talked with them, they couldn't help but stay around.

---

3. Yancey, P. (1997). *What's So Amazing About Grace.* Grand Rapids, MI: Zondervan.

CHAPTER 1: WHERE DID WE GO WRONG?

COURSE CORRECTIONS

As we look at creating a culture of grace, some of our beliefs can actually get in the way. Or, I should say, the way we hold and live out these beliefs gets in the way. We believe, "Jesus saves! God can change you! Be transformed!" These beliefs are right. They are true. They are easy to say and preach, but harder to live. If we are being honest, we know that it usually takes a while. These are "process" words—salvation, change, transformation. They can have an "instant" beginning. We say a prayer, so we are "saved," but to fully experience them takes time. We forget this: we get into church mode and start to expect the gathered souls to be "formed" and "processed" already. So we're surprised when someone isn't fully saved, changed or transformed; and our inability to create space for this process gets us in trouble.

We can make allowances for unbelievers, who can come "messed up," but then we expect them to get saved and be transformed. Truth be told, in our churches, we want people who are processed and mature already. The reality is that most of us, maybe all of us, are still in process and *becoming* mature. This can be messy, but without this expectation of messiness we will never have grace. Grace always has a messy side because if there isn't a mess, we don't need grace.

If a culture of grace is a path we take, then we need to honestly assess the map and see where we have taken the wrong path. Consider the following paths that lead away from grace, and try to honestly assess if you can identify with any of them.

How we react to sin and confession. On the occasion that someone confesses to sin (or more likely gets caught in it) our reaction speaks to the kind of culture we have. In my opinion, these are some of the wrong reactions we can have as a church.

- We react in shock, surprised that they, or anyone in our church, would be doing such a thing.
- We have an attitude of self-righteousness, or even worse, a smug satisfaction that we would never do such a thing, therefore we are experts at fixing them.
- We rank sins or habits, and treat some severely while seemingly ignoring others. Or we might say something like, "We don't talk about that here," refer them to a professional counselor and end the conversation.
- We hush them up, and say, "Well, never do that again!" We might even make them promise us, or the whole church, that they won't.

Reactions to sin such as these will never take us on a path toward becoming a grace culture.

Believing that change is simple. Another wrong path is to act as if change is simple; only a matter of deciding to change. Maybe we don't say as much but our actions betray us. We give the person struggling with sin a few verses to read and tell them to pray more, assuming this will fix the problem. Now, prayer is powerful and the Word of God does change lives, but this counsel isn't a magic cure. If changing our bad behavior was as simple as making a choice to never do it again, no one would struggle with sin. We would simply say to God, others or ourselves, "I will never do that again!" and we would be free. How many of us have said that a million times about a million different faults, and yet we find ourselves back again? Change isn't simple, and when we act like it is, we become a performance-based culture, not a grace-based culture.

CHAPTER 1: WHERE DID WE GO WRONG?

Church discipline that emphasizes punishment instead of restoration. When a believer is caught in serious sin that requires some level of church involvement, we unintentionally (or intentionally) communicate to the person, "Shame on you. Now you have to pay and really be sorry before you can be one of us." This not only communicates how bad they are, but how good the rest of us are in comparison. The process can ostracize the person and leave them feeling like they must wear a scarlet letter until they have paid penance. But the purpose of church discipline is always restoring the believer to full fellowship. This process will include some required action on the part of the person under discipline, but these actions must always be about restitution (paying back so they mature) as opposed to punishment (paying *for* so they learn their lesson).

Taboo topics. What we don't talk about as a church says more about us than what we do talk about. When we have taboo topics that no one discusses—either from the pulpit or in small groups—we communicate that we don't know how to handle these topics, or even worse, that God's grace doesn't extend to them.

I once met with a guy for coffee, and during the course of our conversation, he was very honest with me about areas of sexual struggle in his life. He had heard me talk openly about similar struggles, even from the pulpit, which made him courageous enough to share with me. What he said typifies what many of us experienced in church culture; "We just didn't talk about this in church. We never did. Everyone knew that everyone else was struggling with real issues and problems, but whenever it came out, we would all act surprised. So no one ever talked about real stuff. I'm so glad we can talk about the real stuff at this church!" His joy and enthusiasm was such an encouragement to me as a leader.

What aren't you talking about as a church? As a family? Are you trying to sweep it under the rug and act like it doesn't exist? Do you avoid certain topics in order to keep everyone happy? That isn't grace!

Only telling the happy stories. Sometimes a church service can suffer from what I call the *"Chicken Soup for the Soul* syndrome." Did you read any of those books? They were compilations of stories that left you feeling good all over. Church can sound like this. Every story has a happy ending. Every problem is fixed, every sickness healed, and every marriage restored. These can be great stories of God's redemption and grace.

I am not against happy stories, but are they the only ones we tell in our sermons? Are the only people we ask for testimonies those with a happy ending? If so, we inadvertently paint the picture that God will always make it better. And if we're not better, then something must be wrong with us.

God IS always at work to make us more like Him. I wholly believe that following Him does make life better, but not always in the way, or in the timing, we would like. What about the marriage that doesn't seem to be getting better? The sickness that is getting worse, not better? The reality for the vast majority of us is that life includes messiness and struggle. Cultures of grace will make room for telling some of these stories.

Honoring the finished product and not the process. Similar to only telling happy stories, this path is all about celebrating the happy people. So, people who are gifted at preaching and playing music should use those gifts, but what about those younger believers who are developing their gifts? Is there room in your church for someone to do an "okay" job because they are still learning? Or do we essentially send people away to learn in private until they are good enough—a finished product?

CHAPTER 1: WHERE DID WE GO WRONG?

I am not saying we should ignore bad preaching and pretend that tone-deaf Susie really can sing. What I am saying is that a culture of professionalism can kill grace. Honoring married couples, graduations, and healed lives is fine; but what about recognizing singles who are learning to live in holiness, students struggling through a program, or honest hearts walking through recovery? If we honor those who are in process, we encourage everyone that it's okay to not be okay.

Replicating the dysfunction of the home. This one is difficult to summarize in a paragraph, because it may open many unanswered questions. I believe that many pastors, leaders, and parents run their current church, ministry, or family like their family of origin. The model they were handed in a dysfunctional human family dominates the way they run the church family, rather than looking honestly at how a healthy family should function. The body of Christ is intended to be a "new family" that can re-parent all of us in areas such as communication, sexuality, conflict resolution, and dealing with grief.

Leader or parent, will you take a moment and honestly assess if you have brought the dysfunction of your family of origin into your new family? If the Spirit brings to mind any area, confess it and ask for help to lead a new kind of family in God's way.

A faulty view of transformation. Somewhere in the Reformation, I believe we adopted a knowledge-based approach to transformation. This view says that if people only know enough truth, they will be changed and live differently. This might have made sense in an era when very few people had a Bible, and the middle-ages Catholic church was veering away from biblical truth. Since that time, colleges and seminaries have flourished as a way of educating Christ-followers, especially leaders, toward transformation. I am one who benefited greatly from my college and seminary years, but training the mind with the Word of God isn't the same thing as shaping the heart by the power of God.

Knowledge can help, but transformation will always require *an experience of healthy relationships.* Knowledge alone puffs-up, but love—relationship with God and others—will build us up.[4] If your primary approach to transformation is preaching and teaching alone, grace will be limited. Grace must be experienced in loving, healthy relationships.

I am certain that more wrong "spurs" exist, taking us away from the true path of grace. As you read, maybe you could identify with a few of these habits that reinforce a climate of shame. My list isn't meant to be exhaustive, but I hope it illustrates how easily we can stray off path, and how even through doing "good things" we can limit grace.

Perhaps you could see yourself on a few of these paths. Perhaps you could see the church you are a part of, or were a part of, in some of these descriptions. Or maybe you have been the unfortunate recipient of some of this treatment. Whatever the case, the point is not to blame others or point the finger at graceless cultures. The point is to identify where we have gotten on the wrong path, so that we can make course corrections and begin traveling down the path of grace.

Remember, if you're on the wrong path, all the effort and desire in the world won't get you to a better place. You may want a culture of grace. You may be trying really hard to be a culture of grace, but if any of these wrong paths are taken regularly, you simply won't get there. You must recognize the faulty path, backtrack (repent), and head toward the right one.

---

4. 1 Corinthians 8:1

CHAPTER 2
I SEE YOU

When I was growing up, my family would travel around to different churches and camps to put on a concert. It was our own version of the Partridge Family, the Osmonds or whatever family you grew up watching. My dad played the trumpet, the piano and the guitar. He taught my sister to play the trumpet, and helped me learn to play the saxophone. We would sing and perform an entire show. We would go to summer camps and provide the entertainment for the whole week.

There were enjoyable aspects to this family dynamic. I have one older sister, a younger sister, and a younger brother. There are four of us within five years; so we are very close in age. But, other parts of this experience we learned to despise because we had to practice together as a family. Imagine your little sister is annoying you, and your little brother's picking on people. Okay, that's not true. I was always the one picking on people. Then, we practiced at the most inconvenient times, like just before dinner. We were constantly whining, "Why do we have to do this?"

We traveled together to churches and concert locations, and this was before anyone had come up with a brilliant invention called the minivan. At that time, we had a car with three of us in the front row and three of us in the back row. We were in close quarters; close enough that Dad could still reach back and grab those of us who were acting up. "She's touching me!"

Sometimes we were fighting and grouchy the entire drive to the concert. Then, we would pull into the parking lot and Dad would turn around and say, "Now listen. We're going in there, and we are the church service tonight. You need to show some class." It was understood that if you didn't go in there and show some class, you would have to answer to Dad, and it would not be good.

So, whatever was going on in the car stopped when we opened those doors. We would walk into that church, cute as could be, sing our songs and put our arms around each other. After the concert, people would come up to us—probably just like you would have if you came to see us—and say, "That was so wonderful. What a beautiful family." They would tell my parents how lucky they are to have kids like us. And, in my head, something began to click. The thought went, "Okay, this is how you do it. You have one dynamic with the family, and then you hide all of that when you go and do the show; that's what everybody likes."

As an eight, nine, and ten-year-old boy, that thought was fairly innocent. But during my high school and college years, this same thought became a driving force and I learned to play the part. I learned to do whatever got me the applause, the strokes, and the "attaboys," and to hide the things that others might not find so glamorous or good.

In my high school career, I played basketball, football, ran track, played in the band, sang in the choir, and participated in student government; at one point, I was even involved in the Young Republicans. (My apologies to my liberal friends. Solidarity to my conservative friends.) I did everything I could do because all of it got me noticed and appreciated. However, underneath, was a growing weariness and a sense of, *What if they knew or what if they really understood? What if they saw all the stuff that I see? Better to just keep that inside.*

Maybe you've been there to some extent. Maybe your family wasn't the Partridge Family Singers, but you learned as a child what got the applause, what made Dad notice, what made Mom happy, and what brought attention from the people that you wanted attention from. You learned to project this, to play the part, to do the dance, and to get the applause. But, on the inside, you learned there was a lot that you didn't want others to know. Most of us brought that right from childhood into adulthood and continued to play the part and do the dance; do whatever it was that got you acceptance.

Wouldn't it be great if you could go into a place and know from the beginning that it was okay to not be okay? Where you didn't have to worry who was watching, you didn't have to put on the mask and look the part, and be a part of the show? You could just be who you are and find that was enough? Wouldn't you want to be a part of that place? That would feel safe.

I want to look at what it would take to build that kind of culture in your home, your relationship with your spouse, your relationship with your kids, and your relationship with your parents; what it might look like to build that kind of a culture in a church.

So how do we build a culture of grace? Let's look at a story that is probably very familiar to you. I hope that as we dig into it, you'll see it in a different light. The story can be found in the Bible, in the book of Luke, chapter 19.

Let me set the stage. Jesus is now on His way to Jerusalem. It is the last time that He will be in Jerusalem because at the end of this trip He will be betrayed, put on trial, condemned to death, and nailed to a cross. But a few days before all of that takes place,

He is on a journey. He's on His way to Jerusalem and first comes to a little town called Jericho.

By this point in Jesus' ministry, He had been a teacher, a rabbi, and a healer. He had gained a tremendous reputation and also a tremendous following. So, everywhere He went, there was a large crowd that would follow Him. It was a mob of people moving through the town and, for a little city like Jericho, this was a really big deal. All of these people suddenly flooding the streets, everyone just wanting to see, hear, and be next to Jesus. That's where we pick up our story.

Jesus entered Jericho and made his way through the town. There was a man there named Zacchaeus. He was the chief tax collector in the region, and he had become very rich.[5] Now you might know the name Zacchaeus. You maybe sang the song like I did in Sunday school, and now it will be stuck in your head. Sorry about that, but he's a wee little man and a wee little man is he. You were in Sunday school too; good for you. Thank your parents for taking you to Sunday school.

Zacchaeus had a reputation. Another word you could use is an identity. It's his public persona: what people know about him. His reputation clearly says something about him. In that day and age, to be a tax collector was more than a job—it was a category.

You see, Rome had conquered too many places to take care of the taxation themselves. Their system was to find people among the areas they had conquered, and raise them up to be tax collectors of their own people. Rome would give them authority and soldiers to enforce their law, and then take a hands-off approach when it came to collecting taxes. Rome's attitude was, "As long as you give us what we want, our due, whatever you get

---

5. Luke 19:1-2

CHAPTER 2: I SEE YOU

on top of that is yours to keep." So when we read that Zacchaeus is a tax collector, this is so much more than a title or a job. This is an identity. It's a reputation, because if you notice he's a **chief** tax collector. And, he is **very** wealthy, which means that Zacchaeus had become good at robbing his own people, and that shaped the person he was.

I want to use a little illustration that might help us see some of ourselves in the story. As we talk about Zacchaeus and his identity—for him and for any one of us—there are two sides to our identity: there's the Public Me, and then there's the Private Me. The Private Me is the me that only I see, or those who are close to me know about. The Public Me is what I allow others to see. The Public Me for Zacchaeus is evident to all. He is a tax collector. He is wealthy. He has everything you would want in the physical world, but, for Zacchaeus, the Private Me is probably a hurting guy. He's become an outcast among his own people. He is someone that other Jewish men turn away from and refuse to acknowledge because of the way he has turned against their religious traditions and is working for the enemy. In that day and age, this was a spiritual decision as much as it was a financial one. He had disowned his own people to work for Rome. The Private Me Zacchaeus carried around was not very positive.

Let's continue with his story:

> *He tried to get a look at Jesus, but he was too short to see over the crowd. So he ran ahead and climbed the sycamore-fig tree beside the road, for Jesus was going to pass that way.*[6]

As I mentioned, Jericho is a relatively small town. There's one main road that passes through—the road to Jerusalem—and this mob of people was headed down the street. I don't know about you, but I usually picture the streets lined with the crowd; but I think it's more that the crowd was moving with Jesus. Zacchaeus had run over to the crowd, but he was short, so he was trying to jump up and look over the mob to see Jesus. When everyone turns back and sees who it is that's trying to see Jesus, they give him no room. In fact, if you were to look back to Luke 18, the people in the front of the crowd are pretty aggressive! A blind man was begging for Jesus to heal him, and they tell that guy to shut up. Fortunately, Jesus heard him and heals him. But, if they would treat a blind man that way, how do you think they're going to treat the local tax collector that takes all their money?

Zacchaeus is too short to see over them and when he realizes that's futile, he looks ahead, runs down the road to a sycamore tree and climbs up in it. We don't know from the text why Zacchaeus wants to see Jesus—what is it about Jesus that is drawing him. Is he just curious? Does he think Jesus will do something for him? We don't know. But, we know that he wants to see Jesus.

As Jesus begins to come that way, something truly incredible happens. Look at verse 5.

---

[6]. Luke 19:3,-4

CHAPTER 2: I SEE YOU

When Jesus came by, he looked up at Zacchaeus and he called him by name. "Zacchaeus," he said. "Quick, come down! I must be a guest in your home today."[7]

You have to really picture this in your mind. Take it out of the Sunday school flannel board and try to get into your heart what's happening. This mass of people is going through town and Jesus is in the middle of it all. The people are pressing around Him, talking to Him and asking questions. They are on the way to Jerusalem, their most important city. Jesus' attention is all on the crowd and on His destiny in Jerusalem. But when they get to the base of the sycamore tree, to the optimal place where Jesus and Zacchaeus can see each other, Jesus stops, looks up into that tree, and calls out to him by name. The Son of God—God in a human body as Scripture tells us—sees the man Zacchaeus. And He knows him. He knows everything.

Jesus had a way of looking at people and knowing them. As Jesus looks up to Zacchaeus, there is this intense moment where He locks eyes with Zacchaeus. He doesn't just see a man in a tree; He sees right into his core, into the essence of who he is. Jesus knows in an instant all that Zacchaeus does for a living, all that he's done to others, and all that others have done to him. Perhaps, Jesus sees the way that, as a kid, Zacchaeus was made fun of and ridiculed by other kids because he was too short.

In the first century, to be handicapped, deformed, or misshaped—to be too short—was not just seen as some kind of physical impairment but also spiritual. If you were too short, God was angry at you or your family for sin and so He made you physically different. In fact, the only other place shortness

---

7. Luke 19:5

is mentioned in Scripture is in a list of physical deformities that would prevent a person from going into the Temple (Leviticus 21:20). Deformities weren't seen as a by-product of DNA, as they often are now, but as the result of sin and being unclean.

Zacchaeus had grown up with this his whole life. Was this something he was rebelling against, becoming a tax collector? We don't know. What I do believe is that Jesus looked into the tree and he saw everything. Zacchaeus was undressed, so to speak, to his very core. What an unnerving moment!

I think Jesus held His gaze, so that there was a brief space of time where Zacchaeus had to wonder, "What is He going to say? He knows it all!" But then he heard his name from the Master's lips, *"Zacchaeus!"* Do you know what Zacchaeus means in Hebrew? Zacchaeus means "pure one." Jesus, the King of kings and Lord of lords, looks up and says, "Pure one, come down. I'm going to your house." In fact, Jesus *insists* on it. "I must come," He says.

The word here for being a guest is more than stopping by; it's actually a word in Hebrew or Greek meaning "to stay, dwell, or abide." It might be that Jesus is actually going there to stay the night before going on to Jerusalem. He means to hang around for a while.

He picks Zacchaeus. Out of the whole crowd pressing around Him begging for attention, He picks the swindler working for Rome. In this moment, Jesus sees through to his core. He sees through the Public Me of Zacchaeus, and He even sees through what Zacchaeus would believe is the Private Me, into another part of Zacchaeus that is also in all of us. This is what I would call his core beliefs: what he believes about himself. Notice in our diagram that follows how our Private Me is composed of two parts—how we see ourselves, and what we believe is true about ourselves.

What Zacchaeus has going on in this areas of life, in his core beliefs, is a conviction that "there is something wrong with me."

God made me short. God has judged me. God is angry with me because of the choices I've made and the person I am.

But Jesus sees into these core beliefs and knows that these beliefs are being driven by lies. Zacchaeus is living out the lies he believes about himself. Then, in one beautiful moment, Jesus sees through the lies and expels them when He says, "Zacchaeus, I see you. I see everything about you, and I want to come stay at your house."

In the first century, to stop by someone's house was more than hospitality. To enter into someone's home, particularly to be a guest there, was to say, "I affirm all that you are. Your reputation can become my reputation. What you're known for, I will be known for, because in coming under your roof, I'm coming under you."

And everyone in the crowd gets it. This is a big moment. Look at how they react.

> *Zacchaeus quickly climbed down, and took Jesus to his house in great excitement and joy. But the people were displeased. "He has gone to be the guest of a notorious sinner," they grumbled.*[8]

---

8. Luke 19:6-7

The public knew Zacchaeus and they said, "Jesus, you don't want to be with him! Do you know what he's done? Do you know who he is?" The crowd has seen Zacchaeus and rejected him because of what they see. Jesus sees Zacchaeus—all of him—and accepts him anyway. What a contrast: the crowd who can only see skin-deep rejects, while Jesus, who can see all the way to the heart, accepts. In going to his house, Jesus is inviting Zacchaeus into a friendship.

This visit has an amazing effect on Zacchaeus. While the crowd is busy grumbling, Zacchaeus is in the midst of transformation.

Meanwhile, Zacchaeus stood before the Lord and said,
"I will give half of my wealth to the poor, Lord,
and if I have cheated anyone on their taxes,
I will give them four times as much!"[9]

Think of the incredible transformation in that moment. Zacchaeus is known for being a wealthy, rich, powerful tax collector. If he's suddenly giving half of it away, and re-paying four times anything he's robbed, he's not going to be a wealthy, rich tax collector much longer! He went far beyond what any law or Old Testament regulation would have asked of a thief.

Why the dramatic change? Because Zacchaeus had experienced Jesus at the deepest level—in his core beliefs. Jesus doesn't start with his public behaviors or even his private image. He went straight to the lies dwelling at the core of his soul.

Now, I'm not saying that Jesus was accepting or condoning what Zacchaeus did, but notice that Jesus never addresses his behavior. Jesus never addresses his sin. He doesn't walk by and say, "Okay Zacchaeus, we need to talk about the way you been living your life." All He does with Zacchaeus is meet him at the

---

9. Luke 19:8

level of his core beliefs and say, "You are worthy of my presence. I want to be your friend." When Zacchaeus experiences this, the stuff that he had been doing fell away. He didn't want it anymore. He didn't need it anymore.

This is the experience of Jesus in our lives. When the lies can be replaced by truth spoken from God, we are changed. Rather than an outside-in kind of change that is based on self-effort and trying harder, change is an inside-out experience of knowing who we are before God. Our behaviors are driven by beliefs. If we attempt to change behaviors but the core beliefs are untouched, we will always run back to the destructive behavior. But when the driving beliefs are purified by Christ's love and acceptance, behaviors can change.

When our core beliefs are informed by truth, then the me is no longer about a Private or Public Me, it's just Christ in Me. Me and Jesus together in true friendship. Zacchaeus didn't need all the other stuff anymore because he had found friendship, and in that acceptance he was transformed. He was changed.

My friends, that's what grace does to us. When we realize we are fully known and embraced by Jesus, sin has a way of falling off. When we are wrapped up in this Public Me and trying to act like we have it all together, we actually sin more. But when we realize in our very core that Jesus knows all the sin, that He is aware of everything, and we let him meet and see us in that place, not only do we sin less, but we really discover what love is all about.

This is the definition of grace. Grace is being fully known and fully embraced by God. In our lives, we often develop a warped perspective that in order to be fully embraced, we must hide all that is not good. We aren't fully known. But because we aren't fully known by God or others, we cannot experience true acceptance. Grace is the beautiful, seemingly contradictory combination of being both fully known and fully embraced.

When that happens, the Public Me and the Private Me begin to disappear until all that's left is Christ in Me. Christ in Me, knowing that I am fully known and fully embraced, not for what I do, but for who I am.

Culture tries to apply grace the opposite way. What culture tries to do is apply grace by looking at the Public Me and the Public You and saying, "You're okay; everything's okay." If you can just believe you're okay, then you can be okay with the Private Me, and if you're okay with the Private Me you don't have to worry about anything else. Culture tries to work this way, only the truth

CHAPTER 2: I SEE YOU

is, it never works! We end up reinforcing the message that we must look, act or perform the way people think we should.

Jesus comes along and He offers grace in a different way. He says, "Let me tell you about who you are. Let me tell you about the value you have apart from any performance. Let me help you understand that I made you on purpose and for a purpose." As that truth begins to form our core beliefs, this dichotomy between a Public Me and Private Me disappears because we find that just me is okay.

Take a look at how our destructive core beliefs can operate in our lives. Let's say that in your core beliefs you carry around an idea like this: people only like me because I'm funny. Because of that core belief, your Private Me feels like "I'm stupid." But, the Public Me—what you put on display—says, "Look at me, I'm funny and outgoing," because that's what makes people like you.

Or, maybe you have a core belief where you doubt that you're worthy of being loved. Because you doubt you are worthy of being loved, your Private Me says, "I'm worthless." But, the Public Me that you show to everyone else is someone who is in control and independent and doesn't really need people anyway.

Maybe at the core of your being you have a belief that says my performance is what makes me valuable, and you struggle with a Private Me that says, "I'm a loser and I'm not good enough because I keep failing in my performance." But on the outside, the Public Me, you're confident and professional.

Can you see how you can't change any of those core beliefs coming from the outside-in? If, at the core of your being, you believe that you're only loved because you perform well enough or because you play some role, then you will never be able to change things on the outside. Jesus comes and speaks the truth that God accepts me for me. He loves me because He created me. It's His love that makes me worthy, not my performance. I'm valuable because I'm His, not because I've done anything to make me valuable. When those beliefs at our core begin to change, then the Private Me and the Public Me disappear and all that's left is Christ in Me. When that happens, grace is being felt and experienced.

By now you're probably wondering—what does this have to do with creating a safe place; a culture of grace? Here's the key: **A shame-repelling culture of grace begins with me**. As long as I believe I have to do the song and dance to be loved and accepted, I am going to project that same belief on to you and perpetuate a climate of shame. You'll be led to feel the same way. But when any one of us experiences truth that transforms our core beliefs, and we get rid of this dichotomy between the Public Me and Private Me and there's just Christ in Me, then we have a way of giving others that same permission. We have a way of passing on grace.

Let's take a look at how the story of Zacchaeus ends.

> *Jesus responded, "Salvation has come to this home today for this man has shown himself to be a true son of Abraham. For the Son of Man came to seek and save those who are lost."*[10]

Zacchaeus was lost. Lost trying to find his identity in accomplishments and power that being a tax collector gave him. But, in Christ, he discovered he was a true son of Abraham. For so many years had he heard the Jews look at him and say, "You're no son of Abraham. You're a traitor! You're not one of us. You're an outcast." And then, Jesus walks into his life and says, "Here's Zacchaeus, let me tell you about him. He's a pure one. Let me tell

---

10. Luke 19:9-10

you something else, because of the way he let me in—let me love him—he's a true son of Abraham."

Zacchaeus' life was transformed in a moment. I would love to know what happened when a transformed Zacchaeus began to walk the streets of Jericho, because someone who has experienced grace has the tendency to give it away. Even radically. They can give back four times as much as what they once took away.

How does this happen? How might this happen for you and me? I see three ways that you and I can begin to experience this kind of grace so that we might build a culture of grace around us.

1. ALLOW YOURSELF TO BE SEEN BY GOD.

Zacchaeus had this moment where Jesus looked up in the tree and knew everything about him. For some of us, if we stop and think about it, this is one of our greatest fears. The thought that God would look inside and see all of me can be terribly unnerving. We feel exposed in the worst way and this makes us want to run and avoid God. We struggle to pray, because to pray means to bring myself into His light, and the light can hurt the eyes of our soul.

It's really a funny thing we do, because if we do stop and think about it, we realize He already knows it all. God has been there; He's seen it. He's more aware of our stuff and our issues than we are. But the question is, "Have we stepped into that place long enough to feel it?" He knows everything. He's seen the hurts I've caused and the hurts done to me. He's seen the way I've broken His heart, and the way others have broken my heart. He knows. But in the fullness of His knowledge we are able to experience the wholeness of His embrace.

Why not take a few moments right now? Close this book, lean your head back, and allow the Holy Spirit to walk with you through your life. Become aware of His gaze on every hurt, every secret, and every fear. Feel the depth of His knowledge of you. Then, hear Him call you by name. Not the name calling you've heard from your past. Hear Him call you by your true name. He calls you Loved One. He calls you Cherished One. He calls you Mine. Can you hear Him?

When we let Him into that place where we are willing to be seen and feel the discomfort of being so exposed before Him, it can bring us to this second way of welcoming in a culture of grace.

2. BEGIN TO IDENTIFY THE LIES.

Only after we are exposed before God and allow Him to see everything can we ask the hard question, "God, what lies do I believe about myself?" We are asking Him to help us see how all of our stuff has led us to false beliefs about our identity. In that place of uncomfortable closeness before God, those lies begin to bubble up about our value, our worth and what makes us important.

This can be a very challenging process, and one rarely accomplished alone. A good method for identifying lies at your core is to make a list of your top ten most painful moments from before the age of 18. Walk through this list with a trusted friend or counselor and look for the themes. What have your experiences led you to believe about you? What lies have been embedded in your soul because of the pain? How did you learn to cope with the fears and failures of life? These themes will point us to the lies. Remember, no matter how we act on the outside, what we believe about ourselves on the inside is the true seat of action and behavior.

As we review our history and begin to hear all those lies, we might be tempted to say, "Oh, God, how could you love me? You must certainly reject me because of these things." But exposing the lies takes us instead to His grace and the third way of creating a grace culture.

3. ALLOW CHRIST TO REPLACE THE LIES WITH HIS TRUTH.

As the lies surface, try to see how God holds the exact opposite view of you. In allowing God to replace the lies with His truth, we are accepting friendship with God. We are accepting friendship with God in the deepest meaning of the word friendship. In its purest sense, a friend is someone who knows everything about you, but still just wants to be with you because they like you. If you've ever had a friend like that, I'm guessing they are a lifelong friend because, with them, you feel something that you don't feel anywhere else.

In your life, imagine if God was this friend; not some judgmental figurehead but the truest of friends, a million times better than you've ever known. He knows all of your stuff and all the lies that you've listened to. But instead of condemning you for believing the lies, He looks you in the eyes and says, "I know you. I made you. Your name is Chosen, Faithful, Worthy and Loved. Look at who I made you to be."

At some point in our life, I wonder how many of us prayed a sinner's prayer and were told that we had become friends with God, but the friendship stayed only surface-level. We think, "God forgives me of my sins—the bad things I do—but, I don't really know what's going on at my core; the things I believe about myself." The truth is, God doesn't just forgive the stuff you do. God forgives who you have become. He doesn't just forgive your sin. He forgives the fact that you are a sinner. "I know who I made you to be and, with My help, we're going to move in that direction." This kind of forgiveness changes our identity.

You see, friendship with God at this level leads to transformation for you and me. We don't sin less because we worked so hard to stop sinning and act a certain way. We begin to sin less because we learn to live out of who God has made us to be, who God has said we are. Grace is being fully known and fully embraced by the God who made us on purpose and for a purpose. As we learn to trust that purpose—that view of ourselves—we cannot help but become more like Him.

TWISTED THINKING

Sometimes in my role, I find that I can get nervous because I often meet new people. I meet new people who come to visit our church for the first time. Or I meet someone for counseling. Or, on occasion, I have a chance to travel and speak at other places and I meet a whole crowd of new people all at once. In these interactions, many fears begin to bubble up for me because I worry about what will make me acceptable to them.

I find myself thinking, "Oh man, I should act older because they probably expect a pastor to be older. I look kind of young, and so how can I appear to be older than I am?" Or I will think, "Boy, I need to be wiser. I'm probably supposed to be really, really wise. I should say wise things. If I say wise things, they'll like me." Other times, I say to myself, "I should have tucked in my shirt. I need to be more professional. I should have worn slacks. I need to act more professional so I will be accepted."

CHAPTER 2: I SEE YOU

The problem with all these reactions isn't if I should be older, wiser, or more professional. The issue is that I feel *the need* to act like I am something that I'm not. When you read that story, you probably find yourself thinking, "No! Just be yourself. That's all anyone wants. Just be yourself." Have you ever noticed how easy it is to say that to others, but how hard it is to say it to yourself? We want others to "just be natural," but when the tables are turned, we hear all the fearful thoughts of rejection: "If I act like myself, do you know what they would say or what they would do?" So if we struggle to say it to ourselves, maybe instead we could learn to hear God say it. He could say, "Just be the person I created you to be, and that's enough. You don't have to show some class, have it all together, or be good enough for Me."

There is an old prayer that says, "God, help me to see what you had in mind when you created the original me."[11] Between God's creation of us and the present moment, a heavy burden of other stuff has glommed onto our lives and we mistook it as our identity. "This must be who I am," we think. But God, in His grace, wants to come in and remove all that baggage and say, "No, no, no, no, no. Who I made you to be is good with Me. Would you just be yourself?"

And as we walk in that grace of being fully known and loved by Him, not only does our stuff have a way of falling off of us, but we begin to create that culture of grace everywhere we go.

---

11. Roberts, T. & Roberts, D. (2010). *Sexy Christians Workbook: For Individuals, Couples, and Small Groups.* Grand Rapids, MI: Baker Books.

CHAPTER 3
THE WORST BEST DAY

I grew up hunting in the hills of Wyoming. More truthfully, I should say I grew up walking with my dad and his family while they hunted in the hills. We moved away before I was ever old enough to carry a gun. In high school and college, I played football all fall and never got back into hunting. After a 27-year hiatus, I finally had the opportunity to go to Wyoming for a deer hunt, and this time with a gun! I was fortunate enough to shoot my first deer ever; a pretty proud moment and one I was so happy to share with my dad.

My plan was to take the meat back home in a cooler as an extra checked bag because that was the cheapest way to get it from Billings, Montana back to Portland, Oregon. A family friend had helped me get the meat processed, packaged, frozen, put in a cooler, and secured with layer upon layer of duct tape.

At the airport, I put my suitcase on the scale first. I don't know how many of you do this, but I really like to check out the little counter on the side that shows how much each bag weighs. I like to know that I can get as close to that 50-pound limit as possible. My suitcase weighed in at 49 pounds and I'm like, "YES! Perfect." The airline attendant took that one off, and I put the cooler on the scale. I watched as the little counter increased and stopped at 53.9 pounds. Oh no! In that moment, it occurred to me that I hadn't actually weighed the cooler ahead of time. In my head, I had calculated the weight of the meat according to what I thought it would be, but I had never actually weighed the cooler once it was full. I was almost four pounds over. The ticket agent gives me a strange look and says, "Well, is there anything we can take out of it, sir?" I said, "It's all packaged deer meat." I looked over at my uncle who is with me, dropping me off at the airport. Ironically, he's a vegetarian.

He hadn't been on the hunting trip. He had just come to see us and help me get to the airport. I'm picturing telling my vegetarian uncle to take home 4 pounds of meat! What's he going to do with that? Then, I'm looking at the duct tape, and it's so securely packed. I ask the ticket agent if he has scissors, and if I open it can he help me duct tape it again. He says, "Well, yeah. We can help you with that." And then he says, "Or..."

Yes! There's an "or!"

"Or, you can check it through as an extra heavy bag," he says.

This is not what I wanted, because I had seen online that an extra heavy bag was very expensive. But then he went on, "And I could waive the fee for that today."

"YES!" I'm thinking, "Why didn't you just say that from the beginning?" Here I was sweating and figuring out what I was going to do with four packages of frozen deer meat, and he's ready to just check it through. I was so happy to get that cooler on the plane and home for no extra charge.

As I was walking toward the security gate to say goodbye to my uncle, I said to him, "Man, it was so nice to get a little bit of grace today."

CHAPTER 3: THE WORST BEST DAY

There's something about grace that we know is important, but perhaps we don't understand or truly grasp what it is. So what is grace? Is grace just having 4-pounds of frozen meat over-looked at the ticket counter? Is grace a physical trait, like the athleticism and agility of the ballet dancer? Is it grace when someone's in a good mood and maybe gives you an order of french fries on the side for free? Is that grace? Or, is it perhaps something more?

You see, if we ever hope to become a safe place and create a culture of grace around us—whether at church, work, school, or at home—we'll need to have a firm grasp of what grace is all about.

As I've already noted, people that were very far from God—the tax collectors, the sinners, those that were notorious for being separated from the Jewish religious system because of their flaws—they were most attracted to Jesus. Why was that? In our day and age, those who feel very far from God stay very far away from the church. How is it that we have lost so much?

Perhaps we have lost sight of what true grace is all about.

How about some definitions of grace that are happening around us right now? How does culture define grace? Simply put, I think culture defines grace by saying, "You're okay, and I'm okay. You do what you want to do, and I'm not going to judge you. Who am I to say it's wrong?" Culture's idea seems to be that we should all do whatever we want to do, and not tell anyone else that what they do is wrong. As long as no one gets hurt, and everyone involved has given their permission, it's okay. In fact, it seems that in our culture, we have made an idol of permission. As long as it's permissive, as long as everyone involved said yes, and we're not hurting anyone, it's okay. Is that grace; just to call everything okay? You're okay. I'm okay.

We have a second definition of grace that we find in religion—whether it's Christian, Hindu, Jewish, or any other kind of religion. Religion tries to say, "I'm okay because I follow the rules, and you are not okay because you don't follow the rules." Isn't that the case in religion—again, whatever religion were talking about—that they tend to have a certain set of rules that are really the important ones to follow? And, I can say that I'm okay because I'm following these really important rules. Yeah, pay no attention to all these other rules over here that I'm not following, but the important ones, I'm following those and you're not. So, I can judge you and say you're not okay, but I am okay. In this case, grace is offered to anyone who looks, sounds, and acts like I do. We look at that definition and say, "Well, that lacks grace almost completely."

Between these two pendulum swings—a permissive, cheap grace and a selective, performance-based grace—we find Jesus. What did He say about grace? Not only that, but how did He act? What might we see in the way Jesus lived? I want to take a look at a passage that I think tells, in a story form, how Jesus approached grace. This story is found in the gospel of John. All four gospels—Matthew, Mark, Luke and John—tell stories from the life of Christ, but it's only in John 8 that we find this unique story.

In this passage, Jesus is in the middle of His ministry and He's in Jerusalem. That's important, not only because it's the center of the economy, government and culture, but it's also the center of religion because the temple is in Jerusalem. The temple is at the center of the Jewish religion because it is the place where the Spirit of God dwells. If you wanted to meet with God in the first century, you would go to the temple in Jerusalem; that's where sacrifices took place, where the law was taught, and where the law was kept. It was the center of their understanding of God. It's at this place that we find Jesus teaching in John 8.

CHAPTER 3: THE WORST BEST DAY

Jesus returned to the Mount of Olives, but early the next morning he was back again at the Temple. A crowd soon gathered, and he sat down and taught them. As he was speaking, the teachers of the religious law and the Pharisees brought a woman who had been caught in the act of adultery.[12]

Here, we are introduced to two sets of characters: the teachers of the law and the Pharisees. We don't know how many of them there are, but I would assume a decent sized group because it doesn't say a teacher of the law or a couple of teachers of the law or a couple of Pharisees; it's a group of them. In that day, everyone would have known who they were because of the way they dressed and the prominence with which they held themselves.

In a culture driven by religion, these were the elites. The teachers of the law were the ones that were the authority on what the law said and how the people were to act. The Pharisees were the ones who walked around making sure all the people did what the teachers of the law said they were supposed to do.

So, they were kind of the heavies. They were the religious elites, and they taught the Word of God because no one had a Bible. The people didn't have an app to go to. They only had what they heard from the Pharisees. And remember, what does religion say? Religion says I'm okay because I follow the law, and you're not okay because you don't follow the law; and, they have with them a prime case—someone who wasn't following the law—a woman caught in the act of adultery.

How she was caught "in the act" we don't know. We aren't given the details, and it's probably better that way. But what is clear is their intent. They are not compassionate about this

---

12. John 8:1-3

woman. They are not trying to help her. They are trying to make a point with Jesus.

The Old Testament law said that if you saw someone about to break the law, it was your responsibility to stop them from committing that sin. So, the fact that they've caught this woman in adultery probably means they were camped out waiting for it to happen. We also know from the Old Testament law, that they had to have at least two witnesses whose stories aligned. If you start to read into that, and think through how such a circumstance would have occurred, this is just a bad situation. They have set up this woman in the most private of settings. They don't care about her; they just want to set up Jesus and undermine His version of grace.

A MODERN TAKE ON AN OLD TEMPTATION

I want to make a quick observation about something that we are still tempted to do today. Because they are experts on the Word of God, the scribes (teachers of the law) and Pharisees think they have the right to take the Bible and punish someone that is not obeying what the Bible says. In doing this, they misunderstand the purpose of the Old Testament law.

The Old Testament law was given to the people so that they might understand their shortcomings. But more than simply understanding their shortcomings, the intent is that they would long to go to God to make things right; that they would sacrifice, worship, pray, and bring their grain and animal offerings, so that they could be made right with God and restore themselves to that covenant relationship. That was the purpose of the law: to bring people back to a covenant relationship with God.

CHAPTER 3: THE WORST BEST DAY

Sure, there are prescriptions in the law about how to punish and how to reprimand, but these were meant to keep people in community. The result of punishment was meant to be a community of people more wholly committed to staying in covenant relationship with God. But, the teachers of the law have twisted this law to be a weapon: because they keep it, they can condemn and punish those who don't. They fell into a trap just as we can. The purpose of God's Word is not to become a weapon that we use to punish and condemn those who we believe are not keeping it. I bring this out because their hearts are not in the right place in this story. Anytime we use the Bible to punish someone for not obeying the Bible, we do the same thing. Now back to the story.

Look what happens next:

They put her in front of the crowd. "Teacher," they said to Jesus, "this woman is caught in the act of adultery. The law of Moses says to stone her. What do you say?"[13]

Here's an interesting tidbit of the Old Testament law that's worth noting: the only place in the Old Testament law we find that someone caught in adultery was to be stoned is if it was a person who was engaged to someone else and then went and had an affair—committed adultery—with someone else.[14] In that instance, in the Old Testament law, both the person who was engaged and the person with whom they committed adultery, were to be stoned. So, there is an obvious absence in the story,

---

13. John 8:3b-5
14. Leviticus 20:10—The verse actually does not say "stoned," but simply "put to death." This is yet another example of how these Pharisees are twisting the law for their own purposes.

right? Simply put, where's the dude? There should be one, because if she was worthy of being stoned, it was with another person and both should be present.

Even though the teachers of the law and the Pharisees are clearly skirting the law, they still have the audacity to bring up what it says in the law of Moses. Remember where they are right now; they are in the shadow of the temple where Jesus is teaching. They are saying to Jesus what the law says—everything their culture is built on—and it says stone her. What do you say?

They were trying to trap Him into saying something they could use against Him, but Jesus stooped down and wrote in the dust with His finger.

They're trying to trap Jesus because they think they've got Him between a rock and a hard place. If He says, "Oh yeah, the law of Moses says stone her—go for it!" then He'll lose the crowd. The crowd is there because of His words of compassion, love, forgiveness, the new kingdom of God and new hearts. If He says to this poor woman, "Stone her," His message will be completely undercut.

On the other hand, if He says, "No, no, no. You don't have to follow that anymore; don't stone her. I'll give you a new law," then they have the authority in their religious system to stone *Him*. They are rubbing their hands together, "We've got Him in our fingers. What's He going to say?" They're watching Him with bated breath, and He stoops down and starts writing on the ground. We don't really know what He wrote, but we know it makes them upset. Look at verses 7 and 8.

They kept demanding an answer.

They are thinking, "Come on! Come on! What are we going to do? Here is the woman. Everyone's watching. You're writing in the dirt. What's going on? Give us an answer!"

CHAPTER 3: THE WORST BEST DAY

It continues, ...*so, he stood up again and said, "All right* (another translation adds "stone her"), *but let the one who has never sinned throw the first stone!" Then he stooped down again and wrote in the dust.*

Here we stumble upon Christ's definition of grace. In this paradigm that I've been creating where culture says, "You're okay, I'm okay, everything's okay," and religion says, "I'm okay because I follow the law, but you're not okay because you don't follow the laws that I think are important," Christ says, "None are okay, but I can make you okay."

Jesus says, "No one is okay." What He's highlighting in the Pharisees is that they are seeking to punish and condemn the woman and put all of the attention on looking her over and writing her off but ignoring themselves. Jesus exposes this flawed system by saying, "Hey, if you're without sin, go ahead and throw the first stone." And everyone in the circle knows immediately they can't throw their rock. They're not okay—they also have sin worthy of judgment.

I want to illustrate what I think Jesus is bringing out in this passage in a way that helps us apply it to our daily lives. The truth is, every single one of us lives under some system of law. We might not call it law; we might think of it more as morality or a sense of right and wrong. But, every single person has some kind of law. We might say, "It's the Bible. That's my law." We might say, "It's whatever the government has passed; I follow that law." Or, maybe it's our own version of right and wrong. It's like, "The law of Joe: whatever I think is best, I'll do that." We all have some kind of law written on our hearts—a belief that this is the way we ought to live.

The challenge in this is that we all break our own law! Whether it's the law of God or the law of the land or the law of Joe, we can't live up to our own sense of right and wrong, can we?

Is there a single person that could say, "All my life I've kept the law perfectly," whether it's the Bible or government laws or just our own? No, we'd all say, "Yeah, I break the law."

When we break our law, we would say that is sin. We might not use that word—some say it's out of date—but sin is a transgression. It's a breaking of the law; particularly, a breaking of God's law. If that word makes you uncomfortable, think of it as "missing the mark." All of us can relate to areas in our life where we have missed the mark.

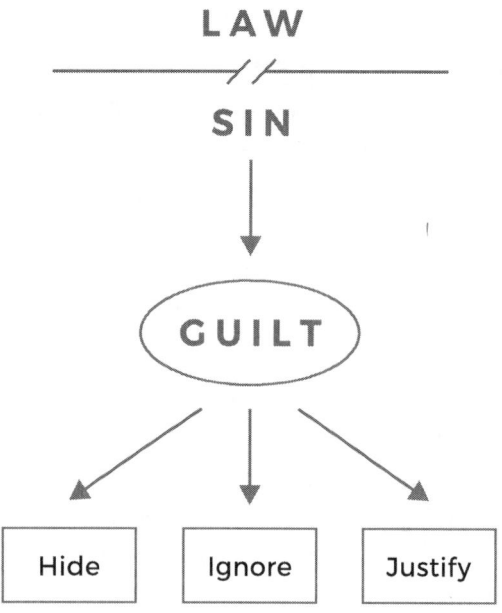

So there's law, and we break our own law which creates sin. When we sin, it produces a feeling or emotion in us, right? That feeling or emotion is called guilt. We feel bad about what we've done. The fascinating thing is that no one had to teach us this feeling. No one had to train us. "Okay, when you do something wrong, you need

CHAPTER 3: THE WORST BEST DAY

to feel guilty about it." We may have been trained about what was right and wrong, but no one had to teach us the feeling of guilt. It "happened" to us when we realized we had done something wrong and failed to live up to a standard. If we could remember our first instance of feeling guilt, no one trained us or taught us or prepared us for it. It just happened.

Further, we are designed—our brain is designed—to dislike that feeling. We work very hard to eliminate it. I think there are three common approaches that we take to deal with guilt in our lives.

1. HIDE IT

This is a really common response in religion. Religion creates a standard that no one can live up to; so everyone acts like they are okay. They hide their guilt and issues, and just put on a smile. That's one approach.

2. IGNORE IT

Another approach we might take—this may be just a little more common culturally—is not hiding it, but ignoring it. We feel guilty until we go out and buy a bigger boat or another car or just work a lot of hours or change careers. Or maybe we go shopping, buy a new pair of shoes, or drink a bottle of wine to help us forget the real issue. We try to ignore what's really going on under the surface, and if we just push it down and stay busy, we won't have to think about it.

3. JUSTIFY IT

The third approach is—and I think this is something we all do whether motivated by religion, culture, or as a follower of Christ—we try to justify it. When we continue to break our own law, God's law, or the law of the land and we feel guilty about it, we decide that it's really not wrong after all. The scary thing is that you and I can talk ourselves into just about anything.

If you live with something long enough and you're tired of how it makes you feel, you can either hide it, ignore it, or talk yourself into it. But there's a problem here. Can you see it?

The problem is that all three of these responses are simply a way of dealing with the feeling that was produced, not with the root cause of the feeling. Hiding, ignoring, and justifying are only attempts to work out the guilt, but never solve the problem. The problem is that at our core, we are lawbreakers. All of us.

In John 8, on that day, Jesus is exposing this system. He is exposing the teachers of the law and the Pharisees. They are caught up in hiding, ignoring or justifying their own sin to fix their own guilt; then putting their attention on someone else who doesn't have it right and accusing her of being the lawbreaker.

So, Jesus says to them, "Whoever is without sin, throw the first stone." Then, He stooped down again and wrote in the dust. Now, what's He doing? We don't know for sure, but I think I have an idea. If you disagree, that's fine. I realize it's not written in the Bible, but there's a connection here that I think makes sense.

Jesus is being challenged by the Pharisees with the law of Moses. What is the center of the law of Moses? The Ten Commandments. The Ten Commandments were written in Hebrew, and in Hebrew they are often referred to as the Decalogue. The Decalogue means "ten words," because the Hebrew language is fairly complex. You

CHAPTER 3: THE WORST BEST DAY

can write just a couple of characters and then by adding symbols, dots or dashes above the letters, you create all kinds of complex words. The Ten Commandments could actually be summarized, for the Jewish people, in ten words. If you think back to the Old Testament and the book of Exodus or, if you ever saw Charlton Heston in the movie The Ten Commandments, you may recall how the Ten Commandments were written. By the hand or finger of God.

Jesus, the Son of God, is writing in tablets of sand. I think He's writing the Ten Commandments in His ten words. He's writing, "Murder," "Stealing," "Adultery." The Pharisees and teachers of the law were mad at Him, but they looked over and recognized those words immediately; they had learned them and taught them their whole lives. When they hear Jesus say, "Okay, anyone who is without sin, throw the first stone," they see these commands. They realize, "I haven't lived up to those." So, look at their response in the next verse:

> *When the accusers heard this, they slipped away one by one, beginning with the oldest.*[15]

It would make sense that the oldest would slip away first, because they've lived long enough to know that they haven't kept the law perfectly. They see Jesus even beginning to write the Ten Commandments and they respond, "Oh! I'm out." They drop their rocks and take off. But, then there are the younger Pharisees that are kind of arrogant and cocky thinking, "No, no. I'm going to throw a rock because murder, I've never done that. Stealing, I've never done that. Adultery, I've never done that, but she has."

---

15. John 8:9

Jesus, though, keeps writing, "Honor your father and mother." They reply, "Aaugh, shoot!" They drop their rocks and take off. I imagine there's one young buck that's just become a Pharisee, and he keeps believing, "No, no. I've kept them all." Until Jesus gets to the last one that says, "Do not covet" (don't ever want for yourself what other people have). "Aaugh! Who hasn't coveted?" He throws down his rock and leaves. They realize, in this case, to throw a rock would be to implicate themselves as someone also worthy of being punished and condemned.

Finally, we have this moment when only Jesus is left with the woman. I wonder, as He's bent down writing in the sand, and the Pharisees drop their rocks and begin to leave, if Jesus picked up one of the rocks.

> *Then Jesus stood up again and said to the woman, "Where are your accusers? Didn't even one of them condemn you?"*[16]

The power of this moment is that the only person in the circle that had a right to throw a stone is the one still standing in front of her. I wonder if, just for effect, He held a stone up for one moment.

> *"Where are your accusers? Does anyone condemn you?"*

> *"No, Lord," she said. And Jesus said, "Neither do I* (sound of rock dropping). *Go and sin no more."*[17]

The only person in the circle that had the right to throw the rock says, "I don't condemn you. Now, go and sin no more."

This woman, as horrible as this day began for her, has experienced a significant moment. In fact, it is the best place

---

16. John 8:10
17. John 8:11

CHAPTER 3: THE WORST BEST DAY

she's ever been. The worst of her stuff—all the things in her life she's been trying to hide—have been exposed for everyone to see. Whether she wanted to or not, she was forced to face the truth. How can that be a good thing, you may be wondering?

You see, there's another option when it comes to dealing with guilt when we have broken the law. Another option is that we actually face the truth as this woman did. In facing the truth before God, she finds something that none of the Pharisees found. In facing the truth, in facing Jesus, she finds grace; real grace. Grace and truth always go together.

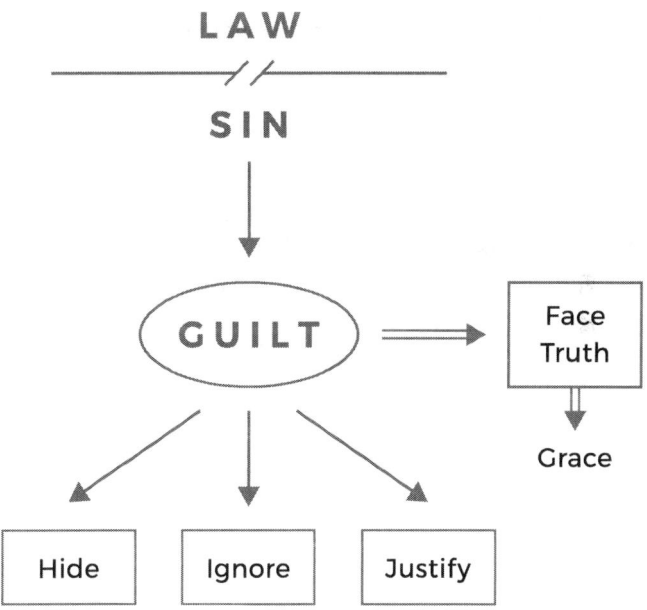

If you're always hiding, ignoring or justifying your actions to try and deal with the guilt, you can't experience real grace. The real issues—the law that's been broken and the sins that have been committed—are left untouched. In truth, the real issues are faced.

The woman caught in adultery faced the truth, albeit unwillingly, but because she did, she was the only person in the circle who experienced real grace.

That's what grace is all about. Grace isn't hiding, ignoring, or justifying any of our stuff. When we do that, we only deal with the emotion or the feeling of guilt. We don't deal with the real problem. Grace is facing the truth before God and others and finding His forgiveness.

Facing the truth—stepping into the light—makes us squint. We say, "Aaugh, I was hoping no one would ever see this. But, it's the worst of who I am. It's the truth of who I am, and here it is." In that place, we can finally and fully hear God say, "I don't condemn you. I forgive."

From time to time, I hear people ask if there is any sin that God either can't or won't forgive. Both Matthew 12 and Luke 12 speak of "blasphemy against the Holy Spirit" as an unforgivable sin, but I will leave the explanation of that phrase to the theologians to sort out for us! I think the record of Scripture is quite clear on confession—*"But if we confess our sins to him, he is faithful and just to forgive us our sins and to cleanse us from all wickedness."*[18] In other words, if we confess it from a sincere heart, He forgives it. If we refuse to confess, and instead willfully choose to hide it, ignore it, or justify it, He can't give us grace. So no matter what you have done or where you have been, if you are willing to come before Him in openness and humility, He will forgive.

---

18. 1 John 1:9

CHAPTER 3: THE WORST BEST DAY

THE OTHERS

Maybe as you read this, you really like the idea of facing the truth before God. But others? Maybe that feels like a step too far. God can be trusted with our stuff; He already knows. But the others, can they be trusted? We wonder, "Couldn't I just take this to God and keep this between Him and me? I'll face the truth. I'll tell Him what I did. We'll deal with it, and He'll forgive me and then I'll be good to go, right?"

The problem is, if we only face the truth with God, we still have the ability to hide, ignore and justify with others. I can continue to hide when I feel like God forgave my sin. I can ignore the impact of it. I can keep talking myself into anything. But, if I will face the truth before God **and others**, in a safe grace-filled community, suddenly I can't hide anymore.

German theologian Dietrich Bonhoeffer, in speaking of our desire to confess only to God and not our brother or sister in Christ, put it this way:

> "Why should we not find it easier to go to a brother than to the Holy God? But if we do, we must ask ourselves whether we have not often been deceiving ourselves with our confession of sin to God; whether we have not rather been confessing our sins to ourselves and also granting ourselves absolution...Who can give us the certainty that, in the confession and forgiveness of our sins, we are not dealing with ourselves but with the living God? God gives us this certainty through our brother. Our brother breaks the circle of self-deception."[19]

---

19. Bonhoeffer, D. (1954). *Life Together: A Classic Exploration of Christian in Community.* New York, NY: Harper & Row Publishers, Inc.

If I start being honest with you, I can't deceive myself any longer. If I start telling others the things I've done, where I've been or what's happening, my ability to justify it goes right out the window. A friend can look back at me and say, "Really? Are you sure about that?" My confession to him draws me into the fullness of God's light. And when that friend speaks a word of forgiveness, God's grace comes to me in a deeper way than when I am alone. Truth suddenly begins to work into grace.

ONE WARNING

This story is such a beautiful picture of the unquestioning acceptance Jesus gives to all those who end up at His feet. However, we must not miss the outcome of grace in this story. Jesus' last five words paint a crystal clear picture of what He believes grace will accomplish in the woman's life: *"Go and sin no more!"*

This leads us to a warning from the passage. The warning is this: grace is not permission. The acceptance we receive through God, and others, is not a cover-up or excuse to continue in evil. Notice that Jesus doesn't say to the woman, "I don't condemn you, either. Go and live as you please." No. In His words to her, Jesus acknowledges that there is a standard. He acknowledges there is a law that is broken when He confirms that sin had occurred.

Jesus upheld that there was a standard of morality—that there were things God has called people to do. He believed that as she experienced His grace, it wouldn't lead to permission but to the power to change. When we experience true grace in the light of truth, it's the kind of grace that changes us. Grace that gives permission isn't really grace at all. The end result of grace is less sin. Not because we work harder at not sinning, but because we learn to trust God's grace and what He says about our value.

CHAPTER 3: THE WORST BEST DAY

In John 8, the woman's sexual sin was an effort to find purpose and meaning that only Christ could give her. But in grace, she received this value. She was empowered to go and sin no more. If we focus on our sin and fixing it, we keep on sinning. If we focus on receiving God's grace, we find our true value and identity in Him. And, by the way, we sin less. We may even sin no more! The *reasons* we sin are being solved by His grace.

If we continue to live with a form of grace that becomes permission, it will leave us not only with the guilt, but with something even worse. We will cover that in the next chapter. For now, let me suggest how we can learn to live in truth so that we might experience true grace.

1. WHERE IN YOUR LIFE ARE YOU HIDING, IGNORING, OR JUSTIFYING?

When it comes to your struggles—your stuff—what do you find is your default mode from these three common reactions? Maybe, as you've been reading about truth, something keeps coming into your mind and you're trying to push it away. You're thinking, "No, not that. I don't want to talk about that." If this is the case, then ignoring might be an issue for you!

As you look at these three reactions, I would encourage you to put a little check mark by your go-to. Which one do you go to most often? Do you hide it, ignore it, or justify it? If the thought of putting a check mark by one of them is nerve-wracking because someone else might see it, then maybe your check mark needs to go next to hiding. Make sense?

It isn't just a few people who should be doing this. It is 100 percent of us; it is all of us. Our fallen human nature is to avoid truth, so we run to these: we hide, we ignore, we justify. What's scary is when we get good at it, we do all three. We hide it from others, ignore it, and if it ever comes up, we justify it away. Sound familiar? It does to me. But if we can acknowledge when we do this, we can begin to build a bridge of truth to the next step.

2. WHAT WOULD YOU NEED TO DO TO FACE THE TRUTH?

What would you need to do to move from hiding, ignoring or justifying to a place of honesty and truth? What's scary to me is that if we don't choose this, sooner or later, it gets chosen for us. Jesus promises us, *"For all that is secret will eventually be brought into the open, and everything that is concealed will be brought to light and made known to all."*[20] Exposure is going to happen; the only question is whether we will choose it willingly, or wait until we have no choice, whether on this side of eternity or before God Himself on the other side.

It's far better to choose truth now and say, "I don't want to live like that anymore. I want to face the truth. I want to take a step." The first step you need to take might be to honestly say to yourself, "I have been justifying this for too long and it simply has to stop."

Or, maybe it's a new openness to God; taking it to Him and saying, "God, I know you already know, but in my strange way of thinking, I've been trying to hide this even from you. God, here it is." Maybe it's talking to someone—a friend or a trusted advisor—and saying, "I just need to share what's going on in my life." Ultimately, facing the truth might mean going to a person that you have hurt or offended and saying, "I have to be honest." What would you need to do to face the truth?

---

20. Luke 8:17

CHAPTER 3: THE WORST BEST DAY

This is where I have found a weekly accountability group, such as a Pure Desire *Seven Pillars of Freedom* group, to be so invaluable. I have found a safe place, where, even as a pastor, I can go week in and week out and be honest about my struggles. As guys in my group offer forgiveness, I am brought deeper into the forgiveness of my Heavenly Father. A Pure Desire women's group can also provide a safe place and the same kind of accountability.

3. WHAT'S STOPPING YOU?

As you look to move out of hiding, ignoring, and justifying, into a place of truth, what is holding you back? Maybe it's fear: fear of what others will think of you; fear of what they might do to you; fear of what will happen if the truth is known. Maybe it's that you don't want to hurt someone. "I know if I tell them about this, they'll be hurt." We continue justifying because of an illusion that says my honesty will hurt them. No, you've already done the thing that hurt them. The fact that you're not telling them is only making it worse. It's not the telling them that will hurt, it's what already happened.

What's stopping you? Maybe it's the embarrassment. Maybe it's the inconvenience of doing something difficult. Maybe you're honest enough to say, "What's stopping me is that I enjoy what I'm doing." If there wasn't some enjoyment in sin, then nobody would sin, right? There's something in it for us. It can be a little bit liberating to honestly say, "I like it. I like when I get mad and yell because then I gain control and I like to feel powerful. Even though I feel terrible about it later, in the moment, I like it." Is there some kind of pleasure, something that we get out of it?

What's stopping you? Would you—in God's grace and God's strength—say, "...but, I'm going to take the step toward truth anyway?" Remember, grace and truth always go together.

A favorite move of mine from the early 1990s is *City Slickers*.[21] In this movie, three New Yorkers fly out to the west to be part of a cattle drive. One day, these three friends—Mitch, Phil and Ed—are riding along on their horses and Mitch says, "All right, best day and worst day of your lives?"

Phil and Mitch both share, and then they get to Ed, "Okay, Ed, your turn." Ed says, "I don't want to play." They chide him, "Come on! We've all shared. It's your turn."

Ed says, "Okay. Fine. Best day of my life was when I caught my dad cheating on my mom again, and I went up to him and I said, 'Dad, we don't need you anymore. I'll take care of Mom and my sister, but you get out.' And he raised a fist like he was going to punch me, and he glared at me, and then he left. And from that day on, I took care of my mom and I took care of my sister."

At this, the friend, Phil, says, "Whew. That's your best day? Man! What's your worst day?" Ed looks back with intensity in his eyes and says, "Same day."

Sometimes, the hardest things we have to do lead to the very best things. Consider the woman in John 8. It started out as the worst day of her life. The thing that she hoped no one would ever find out about was suddenly flung before the crowds and in front of Jesus Himself. Caught in the act—the worst day of her life.

But, in the presence of the Savior, she finds forgiveness. She is empowered to go and sin no more. I would wager that she looked back on this day and said, "Worst day? Absolutely. Best day of my life? Same day."

---

21. Face Production (Producer), & Underwood, R. (Director). (1991). *City slickers* [Motion picture]. USA: Castle Rock Entertainment/Nelson Entertainment.

CHAPTER 3: THE WORST BEST DAY

In the spring of 2011, I made a public disclosure to my church family about my struggle with pornography; a 15-year addiction that I had continually tried to hide, ignore and justify. But by God's grace, I had found lasting freedom through Pure Desire Ministries counseling program. I wanted to share the victory I was experiencing, but I first had to be honest about the sin and the secrecy.

It was a very hard day; it was a very humbling day. I found it gut-wrenching to be so honest and to ask a whole group for their forgiveness. But, if you were to ask both my wife and me about our best day in ministry—same day. In truth, we found grace and love like we had never experienced before. For me personally, I was able to receive love deep in my soul; a place previously hidden from anyone in the congregation because of my sin. In confession, grace rushed in. As a result, we continue to see the fruit in many lives and marriages in our congregation and throughout our community.

I have watched so many men and women courageously follow that same path. They step forward and say, "I'm not going to live in this anymore. By God's grace, I can change." As their honesty opens them up to the grace of God and His power to do what only He can do, they are being set free. I'm so proud to watch that happen.

If you've stepped into this kind of journey, I want to encourage you: don't grow weary. Keep going. Keep stepping into the light even when it's bright and makes your eyes squint. "I thought we dealt with this, but here I am again facing the truth." Keep doing it!

For others, this might be a watershed moment. You realize you need to have a *best/worst day* experience, and some truth needs to come out. Some things need to be faced. It might be hard or messy or ugly or difficult or challenging, but in the truth there will be a grace like you have never known before: a grace that sets you free, a grace that empowers you to understand God's forgiveness at the deepest level of your heart, a grace that enables you to go and sin no more—to live and walk in freedom.

Truth and grace always go together. When we face our truth before God and others, we find the kind of grace that transforms our lives. A culture of grace is a culture of truth.

CHAPTER 4
COVER ME

In this book, we're trying to discover how to become a safe place and safe people; where it's okay to not be okay. A place where we don't feel the pressure or the need to get all cleaned up and dressed up, or to put on a happy face or a performance, so that we can be accepted.

We want to create a place where someone who is very far from God, who feels as unspiritual as anyone has ever been, could walk in the door and say, "I feel at home here." Isn't the opposite more often the truth? On those weeks when things are out of order and there's chaos or conflict around us, something inside us thinks about the gathering with other people—a church, a small group, or a even just our own family—and we fear it. We get the feeling that everyone else has it all together, and we're a wreck. We can't go there because everyone will see what a wreck we are.

If you think about it, this is one of the reasons that bars and pubs are so popular. There's a general expectation in the bar that everyone's life is messed up on some level, and so people gather to have a good time and drink a few brews in the midst of their chaos.

Could a church, a small group, or a family be like that? Okay, not the "escaping life by drinking" part, but what about the freedom to just be who we are in all our mess?

In the story of Zacchaeus, I stated that if we are going to create a culture of grace, it begins with me. To be a culture of grace, we first need to be a person of grace. A person of grace understands that when God looks into their life, He sees it all; yet, He offers us friendship.

In the story of the woman caught in adultery, we saw how important it is to face the truth. Rather than hiding, ignoring or justifying our stuff, we walk into the light and face the truth. When we do, as hard as this might be, we are able to experience real grace in our souls. The cycle of law-breaking can cease because we address the motives of our heart.

Truth is one of those ideas that is really great to talk about. We talked about living in truth and my guess is, as you hear that, something inside you says, "Yes! To live in the truth—to be wide open about who I am—that's what I want to do!" It's great to talk about truth, but then we think about actually doing it. To live in truth means we would need to talk to others about "this." We'd have to be open about "that." Truth starts to feel scary.

Maybe we have started to role-play in our minds what it would be like to face the truth with someone: "Okay, I'm going to sit down with them and I'm going to open my mouth and these are the words I'm going to use to tell the truth about what's going on," and suddenly we're not sure if we want to do that! We hear the lie that it's easier and better if they don't know. It's better that it doesn't come up. It's better left alone.

So where do we get the courage to live in truth? How can we find the courage to live in that place where we're not hiding or ignoring or justifying? A place where we're able to tell God and others, "Here's what's going on; I need you to know because I'd

CHAPTER 4: COVER ME

rather stay in the light, even if it hurts my eyes, than to keep living in darkness." This chapter is all about finding that kind of courage.

Do you have *those* friends? *Those* friends; the ones that talk you into doing things you probably wouldn't have done on your own. They get you into situations that you look back on and they make some great stories, but they didn't necessarily lead to great choices.

I had those friends in my life when I was in grade school. Those were the friends that I would light matches and burn ants with in the back alley. Then, one time, it caught the dry grass on fire, and then the neighbors garage as well, but that's another story for another book. It was those friends that helped me break into the high school track shed. We found two bags of limestone chalk and spread it all over the equipment in the shed. But, another story for another time. Those were the friends that I hung around with growing up.

Growing up, we had a playground, so to speak, in our neighborhood of Greybull, Wyoming. There, in the Big Horn Basin, was this large dike that ran along the river. There was an area between the dike and the river that was an uninhabited "no-man's" land; trees, brush, and wild, unkempt land. It flooded once every bazillion years, so no one worried about us playing back there. It was the perfect place to play all of our games.

The most typical game we would play was a version of capture the flag; two teams against one another with a home base to defend. Only, in our version, it always involved some sort of projectiles to throw at the other team, whether this was rubber band guns, BB guns or little pebbles. We had some general rules about the size of stone that could be hurled at the other team. The object of our game was to protect our base while also trying to discover and "conquer" the other team's base.

We would stalk through the trees and brush, darting and diving, trying to find where the other team had set up their base. Inevitably, a moment would come in the game where, to really figure out what was going on, you needed to move into an open expanse. You knew that you'd be vulnerable and exposed; that you'd be weak because the other team could see you before you saw them. You would turn to your teammates, and say this great phrase that also comes up in every western movie worth watching. You would say to them, "Cover me! I'm going in; cover me!" And, if someone was covering you, if they were covering the weak places or where you felt vulnerable or exposed, you were willing to take risks. You were willing to walk into places that, maybe without that covering, you wouldn't have gone. But because someone had your weaknesses—your vulnerabilities—covered, you went for it.

I wonder, in life, how many of us stay trapped in grace-less, convenient places, unwilling to risk—unwilling to step out to places that require courage or vulnerability—because we're not certain who has us covered.

I want to look at a story in Scripture that reflects where this kind of courage, this kind of covering, comes from. This is a very, very familiar story. It's one that, even if you didn't grow up in church, you know the story or at least think you know the story. This is the story of Adam and Eve in Genesis 3.

> *The serpent was the shrewdest of all the wild animals the LORD God had made. One day he asked the woman, "Did God really say you must not eat the fruit from any of the trees in the garden?" "Of course, we may eat fruit from the trees in the garden," the woman replied. "It's only the fruit from the tree in the middle of the garden that we are not*

CHAPTER 4: COVER ME

allowed to eat. God said, 'You must not eat it or even touch it; if you do, you will die.'[22]

That's a pretty serious warning.

The serpent responds in the next verse: *"You won't die!" the serpent replied to the woman. "God knows that your eyes will be open as soon as you eat it, and you will be like God, knowing both good and evil."*[23]

One fascinating aspect of this story is that Satan takes an approach with Adam and Eve that he continues to take in our lives today. When he slithers into the scene, he doesn't directly contradict God's Word. He doesn't speak a direct lie or the exact opposite of God's command. Instead, he takes God's truth and calls it into question. He causes Adam and Eve to begin to doubt that God is actually good and that God is for them. Do you notice that? The serpent says, "Is that really what God said? Are you sure? Really? He's holding out on you. There's something better out there for you, but He's making you do it His way just because He knows there's something better for you. Is that what God really said?" Seeds of doubt are sown that will later bear the fruit of disobedience.

I bring this up because we face the same kind of temptation in our lives. Satan doesn't try to get us to completely disregard what God said, but plants the idea that perhaps God can't be trusted. Perhaps God's idea of marriage, His ideals of sexuality or standards of obedience, are really God's plan to keep us from something even better.

---

22. Genesis 3:1-3
23. Genesis 3:4-5

C.S. Lewis paints a graphic picture of this in his classic work, *The Screwtape Letters*. In this insightful work, Lewis depicts a veteran demon (Screwtape) sending letters of wisdom to his nephew (Wormwood) on how to tempt and trip-up humans. In one section, Screwtape writes,

> "Never forget that when we are dealing with any pleasure in its healthy and normal and satisfying form, we are, in a sense, on the Enemy's ground. I know we have won many a soul through pleasure. All the same, it is His invention, not ours. He made all the pleasures: all our research so far has not enabled us to produce one. All we can do is to encourage the humans to take pleasures which our Enemy has produced, at times, or in ways, or in degrees, which He has forbidden."[24]

Satan comes and casts doubt on the goodness of God's plan. "Did God really say...?" Now, because their relationship with God has been thrown into doubt, the thought that God might be holding out on them takes root. Because of the temptation that something better is available, if they take it into their own hands and do it their way, Adam and Eve are convinced.

The passage continues: *The woman was convinced. She saw that the tree was beautiful and its fruit looked delicious, and she wanted the wisdom it would give her.* In other words, she bit hook, line, and sinker, into this ideal that there was something better out there for her and that God was holding out on them. She wanted what she could not have, and then...*she took the fruit*

---

24. Lewis, C.S. (2001). *The Screwtape Letters*. New York, NY: HarperCollins Publishers.

CHAPTER 4: COVER ME

and ate it. Then, she gave some to her husband who was with her, and he ate it, too.[25]

It's important to note that Adam was there with Eve. This is a good translation of the Hebrew text because too often, we put all the blame on Eve, "That foolish woman," falsely believing that she caused this problem. Yet Adam is there with her; right beside her—a silent but complicit partner. Unfortunately, he's taking the role that men take far too often. We're present but silent. Maybe Adam's thinking, "There she goes again talking to the animals. Babe, we've got a job to do. We are out here naming the animals, not talking to them." He's just there, silent for whatever reason. When it comes down to the moment of the fall, he's fully participating right next to her. He eats as well.

"At that moment, their eyes were opened, and they suddenly felt shame at their nakedness. So they sewed fig leaves together to cover themselves."[26]

Something fascinating happened in this moment. This point gets missed all the time whenever this story is told. Here it is: An action they took outside of themselves changed the way they saw themselves.

Think about that for a moment; this is so significant to you and me. Something that they did outwardly, an activity that took place outside of their body—an action, an attitude, a behavior—affected the way they saw themselves inwardly.

If you were an outside observer who could step back and just watch this moment happening, it would look kind of foolish to you.

---

25. Genesis 3:6
26. Genesis 3:7

It's silly to think that something they did outside of themselves would somehow affect anything on the inside. They are just as naked now as they were five seconds ago. Nothing about their bodies changed, nothing about their appearance, and nothing inside of them was different. Yet they suddenly felt the need to hide and cover up, because they feared what was being exposed.

While nothing about them had changed fundamentally or physically, something in their brain had shifted. The way they saw themselves had been altered. The significance of this is that all human beings have followed the same pattern since the fall of Genesis 3. The things that happen outside of us—sometimes they are things that are done to us or forced upon us, or the things we choose to do—create a mental image of the way that we see ourselves.

In the last chapter, I said that if we get caught up in cycles where we attempt to hide, ignore or justify our guilt, that guilt doesn't go away. In fact, it morphs into something worse and we see that "worse" occurring right here in our story. Can you see it?

Suddenly they felt shame. Guilt, over something done, quickly turned to shame.

GUILT AND SHAME

Have you ever thought of the difference between guilt and shame? It's more than subtle. Understanding the deep difference between guilt and shame is significant to creating a culture of grace. You see, guilt is a feeling or emotion that says, "I did bad." Guilt occurs when I do anything that I believe violated my standard or God's standard. I broke some rule or law. I did something bad, so I feel guilt over it.

CHAPTER 4: COVER ME

The guilt that goes unaddressed morphs into shame. Shame says, "I am bad." Because of something that happened outside of myself that was bad, I feel guilt. But guilt can wreck me further by leading me to believe that the reason I did bad is because I AM bad. Shame imprisons me through an altered way of seeing myself. In other words, there's something wrong with me.

Once we believe there's something wrong with me, we do exactly what Adam and Eve did—we hide. Adam and Eve hid by literally covering their physical bodies in an attempt to cover up their shame. Our hiding tends to happen more often on an emotional level—hiding from others; or on a spiritual level—feeling the need to hide from God.

This is reflected in the chart from chapter 2. Take a look at our illustration again. Usually, you and I are accustomed to seeing ourselves in two halves: one half is the Public Me—that others see, and the Private Me—that only we, or those we allow close, can see. The Public Me is what I let you see. It's the clothes I wear, the job I have, and the side of me that I'm comfortable with people knowing and seeing on Facebook. It's not all of me, but it's the me that I hope everyone will accept.

The Private Me, again, is that side of me that you don't see unless I let you. It's in this Private Me that I do things, think things, or say things that I'm not necessarily proud of; I don't want you to see that, so it stays private and hidden.

The Private Me can also be divided into two parts: my behaviors on one side and my core beliefs on the other side. Core beliefs are the ideas about who I am. In the Private Me, I carry around what I did. In the core beliefs I carry around who I am.

You might be wondering why we're back on this chart. Stick with me. We're almost to the point. In the Private Me, we carry around these ideas that I did something bad. It's in our core beliefs, at an even deeper level in our brain, that we believe "I am bad." I believe myself to be selfish, unspiritual, rejected, unworthy or any number of additional ideas. These core beliefs, based on lies, are the source of our shame.

Now, here's the problem. Many of us have been taught or we believe that Jesus came to die in order to forgive our sins. This is true; but only partially. What, after all, are sins?

Sins are actions and behaviors, attitudes and thoughts. They all exist in our Private Me that says, "I did bad." This is good news. It's good news that Jesus forgives those sins because I see them and I'm not proud of them. I am happy to know that Jesus would give His life on my behalf and forgive my sins, so I don't need to feel the guilt that I did bad anymore. But, if this is the only place where we meet Jesus, can you see why this is a problem?

At a deeper level, we're still carrying around a belief that I am bad. As long as I believe that I am bad, I will continue to do bad things out of this faulty view of myself. This elementary teaching of salvation can leave me feeling glad that Jesus forgives the bad in my life, but still defeated because I don't know what to do about the places where I feel I am bad. I am saved, but still filled with shame.

Jesus came to forgive sin—yes. But, much more than that, Jesus Christ gave His life on the cross because you and I are sinners. He recognized our fallen human nature that believes shameful things about us. His death was a proclamation to our core beliefs that we are forgiven; not just for what we do, but for who we are apart from Him. As Romans 8:1 declares, "So now there is no condemnation for those who belong to Christ Jesus!"

A shame perspective of ourselves is not typically what we walk around thinking about, "I'm really feeling shame today." But, at a very low level, it's like the background music playing in our lives. This background music can say I'm not good enough or I'm bad, unworthy and dirty. And, just like the music that plays when you are shopping, affecting your mood and how much you buy, this background music affects everything you do.

DEALING WITH SHAME

We have only two options when it comes to dealing with shame in our lives. Adam and Eve have illustrated what happens when we feel shame; we cover up. This is option one when we are feeling shame: **self-covering**. Because I have something to hide, I need to cover it and keep it carefully secured and concealed so that you won't see what it is. In one single moment, Adam and Eve are suddenly in the thick of self-covering. They initiate the world's first-ever game of hide and seek! Take a look at this:

> *When the cool evening breezes were blowing, the man and his wife heard the Lord God walking about in the garden.*

So they hid from the Lord God among the trees. Then the Lord God called to the man, "Where are you?"[27]

Have you learned that when God asks a question, it's not for information? God's not walking in the garden saying, "I could swear they were just here yesterday. Where did they go? Where are you?" God knows what's going on: He understands exactly what's going on. It brings to the surface, in a somewhat humorous way, what you and I try to do. We might scoff at Adam and Eve for thinking they can hide from the Lord of the Universe, but how often do we have similar twisted thinking: "Maybe if I don't tell God about it, He won't know. Maybe, if I don't pray about it or think about it, then God won't see what I've hidden behind the bushes. I can keep it there and go on acting like everything's okay." Something outside of us has changed how we see ourselves, so we attempt to self-cover.

In this story, it would appear that this was God's regular routine. In the evening when the cool breeze starts to blow, God walks through the garden. This happens for Adam and Eve day after day. But on this particular day, God's presence brings fear. Look at what happens:

God called to the man, "Where are you?" Adam replied, *"I heard you walking in the garden, so I hid. I was afraid because I was naked."*[28] In other words, "God, Your presence brought fear because I now have something to hide about myself."

If the way we approach life is to say I've got to cover over things that need to be hidden—option one of self-covering—the

---

[27]. Genesis 3:8-9
[28]. Genesis 3:9-10

CHAPTER 4: COVER ME

warning is this: *shame and fear are inseparable.* Shame and fear are inseparable because if we carry around any pocket of shame, even a small amount in any area of our life, we will fear being exposed. We fear being caught, found out for who we really are, or seen in our nakedness. So, if we live with shame, we will live with fear. There's no way around it.

I don't know about you, but this becomes a strong motivation to deal with the shame in my life. I know the power of fear. I have seen the destructive force of fear at work in my life and in the lives of others around me. If fear dominates my life, it will lead me to choices I never wanted make, to say things I never meant to say, and do things I never intended to do. When we are motivated by fear, we will go in a direction that we don't want to go. Fear drives us to survival and self-preservation. Such a way of life will never lead us to God. What drives the fear is the shame. The good news is that if you deal with the shame, you deal with the fear.

Think about this for a moment: Adam is saying to the God who created him, made him with His own breath and knows everything about him, "There is something shameful about this physical body. I was afraid because I was naked."

We might tend to see this statement through a modern example. We all have these nightmares where we show up at some public place in our underwear, or less, and our response is, "I'd be ashamed too. That's horrible."

But, think of Adam and Eve. In God's perfect garden, as far as we know, they've never interacted with other human beings that would have created any embarrassment over their physical bodies. Adam and Eve's entire frame of reference is one another, and God, in His perfect, unspoiled garden. But one decision against God changes their brain to believe they have something wrong with themselves and they need to hide. This is what shame does to all of us! It tells us, with no logical basis, that we are broken and we had better hide.

I love what God says next. He again asks a fantastic question. (Remember, He doesn't ask questions for information. He's trying to expose what's going on.) God says, *"Who told you that you were naked?"*[29] In other words, "This idea that you need to cover up—that you have something to hide—didn't come from Me. Who told you that you're naked? Who told you there's a problem; something that isn't worthy of being seen? It wasn't Me, Adam. So who gave you this idea?"

The Lord God asked, *"Have you eaten from the tree whose fruit I commanded you not to eat?"*[30] God asks Adam and Eve if they have taken matters into their own hands; if they have disregarded His commands for life, joy, and fullness, and instead believe that there was a better way of their own making. Adam, did you do what I commanded you not to do? And *the man replied, "*(Well Lord), *It was the woman you gave me who gave me the fruit, and I ate it."*[31] Yeah, that's what happened, Lord. It's the woman you gave me—this is her fault. And God, you gave her to me, so really this is your fault! Adam is being driven by fear, and fear will always lead us to place blame on others.

The pattern continues: *Then the Lord God asked the woman, "What have you done?" "The serpent deceived me," she replied. "That's why I ate it."*[32] Adam blames Eve (and God), Eve blames

---

29. Genesis 3:11a
30. Genesis 3:11b
31. Genesis 3:12
32. Genesis 3:13

CHAPTER 4: COVER ME

the serpent, and Satan had no one left to blame! But, Adam and Eve do what we continue to do to this day. When there's any level of shame in our lives, or as soon as something pricks our sense of shame and starts to expose it, we have a predictable response: deflect, deflect, deflect.

"It's not me, Lord. You shouldn't be talking to me, you should be talking to my spouse. The only reason I'm doing what I'm doing is because of what they said or what they did. You need to go talk to my parents. If you saw the way they treated me, or the messages they gave me...it's them, Lord. Go talk to them. Talk to my boss. I would have never done this if they hadn't done that, God. It's them!" We blame and we deflect. We are afraid of being exposed. We are afraid of being seen for what we are. I really believe that in this story, that's all God is trying to do; bring to the surface what's gone on so that He can have a hand in helping restore Adam and Eve. But instead of seeking a restored relationship, they are busy passing the buck.

I want to bring up an important point in what God says next. Collectively, these are often referred to as "the curse." When God talks about the serpent He uses the word cursed. A few verses later, when God talks about the ground, He uses the word cursed. But, when He addresses the people that He's made, He does not call them cursed. I bring this up because sometimes in our modern mentality we think of curses as something vindictive that's spoken against us by someone else, often just to bring unnecessary harm into our life. I wonder if we haven't, in some way, transplanted that idea onto God; God has cursed me. God doesn't use the word cursed when He talks to the man and the woman. I believe what He talks to them about are the *consequences* of what they've done. Sin resulted in a curse, and our sin nature can be seen as a curse, but we have improperly applied the idea of curses to God's relationship with us.

In the Old Testament, when you run across this idea of blessings and curses, it's not God arbitrarily cursing someone because their behavior is bad. It's God explaining how He has created and given us law—this good way—and if we follow it, here's the good that will come. That's blessing. If we don't follow it, here's the bad that will come: the consequence. I would argue that the Old Testament idea of curse, when God uses it with people, is closer to our idea of consequence. God is not out to get you (curse), but He provided for some painful outcomes to our choices (consequences) so that we might turn to Him.

OPTION TWO

Aren't you glad there's an option two? You thought I forgot about the second option for dealing with shame, didn't you? Well here it is. Look at what happens after God finishes dealing out curses and consequences:

> *Then the man—Adam—named his wife Eve, because she would be the mother of all who live. And the* Lord *God made clothing from animal skins for Adam and his wife.*[33]

Think about that picture for a moment. Up to this point in this perfect garden, there has been no sin and no death. Then Adam and Eve sinned. God takes two of His perfectly created animals, we don't know how, but in some way, He slaughters them and the blood of these unblemished animals runs across the ground. He

---

33. Genesis 3:20-21

CHAPTER 4: COVER ME

takes the skin of those animals and places them around Adam and Eve. In this dramatic act, God says to His children, "Let me cover you. You've tried to cover yourself with fig leaves and you feel you have something to hide, but let me take the life of one of my beings and sacrifice that life on your behalf so that I might cover your shame."

This is option two when it comes to how we deal with shame: **God-covering**. God says, "I will cover your shame by the sacrifice of another life. I will wrap that life around you, and your shame is covered." Adam and Eve are sent away from the garden, yes, but they are marked by God. He alone has covered their nakedness and shame.

An often overlooked implication of this passage is the ideal of God's created order. Think about this idea for just a moment: God never intended for you and me to know the difference between good and evil. Do you see that? When Adam and Eve ate of the fruit, their eyes were opened and they began to understand good and evil (as Satan said they would.) Their consciousness became aware of the things they did that were good and other things they did that were evil.

Until that moment prior to their disobedience, they didn't know good and evil. What does that mean? It means that God's intent was not that you and I would know good and evil. This is a result of the fall. God's intent is that we would walk in relationship with Him and trust Him. Adam and Eve had walked each day with God in the garden, and whatever they needed to know, God would tell them. They didn't have a system of good and evil. They just had a trust relationship with God. But because that trust relationship was broken—because they feared that God was holding out on them—it was in that place, they developed shame.

This is so critical to a culture of grace, so please don't miss this: this means that the path out of shame isn't trying harder to please God. The path out of shame isn't to do better at upholding good and avoiding evil. The path out of shame is trusting what God says about you, and that what God says about you is true. Doing good and avoiding bad doesn't eliminate shame. A trust relationship with your Heavenly Father is the only way to destroy shame.

The remedy to shame is not telling people to work harder and avoid doing shameful things. The remedy to shame is trust. Trusting in the covering given to us by God; trusting that what God says about you is more important than anything else.

The truth is, God has covered our shame so that we don't have to hide anymore. What Adam and Eve discovered in the garden and what God is trying to reveal to us through Jesus Christ, is that Jesus didn't come to deal only with the Private Me, where we hide the sins that we've committed that make us feel bad. Ultimately, the cross of Christ is our covering—the covering of an unblemished life and His perfect blood spilled out over the world. His life was wrapped around ours as a divine covering for shame. God is saying to us, "You don't have to be ashamed anymore because I've got you covered. The life of My Son covers your shame. I didn't just forgive the bad things you have done; I've declared that you are not bad. You are Mine!"

We can have the courage to live in truth by realizing that God has covered our shame through Jesus Christ so we don't need to hide anymore. There's nothing to be ashamed of before Him. When our shame is gone, we can actually gain the confidence we need to address sin in our lives.

As we think about applying this kind of grace to our lives and communities, I want to encourage you to adopt two practices.

CHAPTER 4: COVER ME

1. EMBRACE CONSEQUENCES AS GOD'S TOOL IN YOUR LIFE.

Embrace the natural consequences of your actions and behaviors as God's tool in your life. When Adam and Eve sinned in the garden, God brought consequences into their lives that created dependence on Him. He put struggle in their relationship and struggle in their labor. Everything He's saying to us about pain in childbirth, pain of relationships and the pain of work is that this struggle will force us to come to a place of depending on Him. Since the trust relationship between us and God has been broken, He will build into creation a need for Him.

Unfortunately, we sometimes think about the forgiveness of sin like a *get out of jail free card*; "If God's forgiven my sin, why should I have to face any bad outcomes? Shouldn't I be free of the consequences?" One day you will be free of the consequences of sin for all eternity. We will be free from those eternal consequence of sins and live in a new, perfect garden. I can't wait to feel the cool evening breeze!

But, right now, the consequence of our sin is what God uses to bring us back to Himself so that we realize our dependence on Him. Author George MacDonald says it this way in his book, *Life Essentials*:

> Jesus never came to deliver people from the consequences of their sins while those sins remain. That would be to throw the medicine out the window while the man still lies sick. That would be to come directly against the very laws of existence. Yet men, loving their sins and feeling nothing of their dread

> hatefulness, have constantly taken this word concerning the Lord to mean that he came to save them from the punishment of their sins. This idea has terribly corrupted the preaching of the gospel. The message of the Good News has not been truly delivered. Jesus came to work along with our punishment. He came to side with it, and to set us free from our sins. No man is safe from hell until he is free from his sins.[34]

The beautiful thing is that if we understand that Jesus Christ came to cover our shame, we don't have to live in this place of self-hatred or loathing ourselves about being bad, unspiritual, or dirty. If we understand God's covering, it gives us freedom to face our sin, and the consequences. We no longer look for a miracle remedy, but look at our consequences as having a healing effect in our lives. We participate with them, and with the Holy Spirit, in our healing. Through sin, we learn to ask God, "Through these things I have done, how can I learn to depend on You?"

Wherever you're facing consequences, wherever your sin or behaviors have gotten you into trouble, would you look at them and say, "God, through this difficult circumstance—this broken relationship and the hard things I'm facing—how is it creating dependence on You?" This is the first practice of a culture set free from shame.

---

34. MacDonald, G. (2004). *Life Essentials: The Hope of the Gospel.* Vancouver, BC: Regent College Publishing.

CHAPTER 4: COVER ME

2. RECEIVE CHRIST AS YOUR CONSTANT COVERING.

The second practice in overcoming shame is to daily receive Christ as our covering. The Lord God, in the garden, took two animals and their skin to cover the shame of Adam and Eve. In the Old Testament, for the people of Israel, God gave them a covering; when they would bring an animal—the sacrifice, a life given for them—it would cover their sin. Then, God sent Himself in Jesus Christ and His blood covers our sin and shame. It's a covering that we must continue to receive, remembering our trust in God. The enemy of our soul will continue to slither into our life. He will try to undermine our trust in God and get us to believe lies about ourselves and about our Creator. These lies can break our relationship of trust, if we allow it. When trust is broken, shame returns; where trust remains, Christ can cover our hearts and minds with His love.

I love the way author John Lynch says it in his video, *True Faced*. Lynch says, "Even on my worst days, I'm 'Christ in John Lynch!'"[35] Even on my very worst days, my primary identity is Christ and not my behaviors.

I can't tell you how many times I have thought about this idea. Sometimes when I'm driving down the freeway to work, I realize, "I just don't feel like it today." I'm headed into counsel someone, and I don't think I know how to help them. Or, I'm going to preach at a weekend service and I'm thinking, "I don't think I can do it. I can't put on the show. I don't think I have what it takes today." And then I'll hear those words, and I'll say: "Even on my worst day, I am Christ in Nick Stumbo!"

---

35. Lynch, J. (2012, March 13). Two Roads. Trueface. Retrieved from https://www.youtube.com/watch?v =Rfyo3PEVUhQ

When I hear that, it changes everything about my mindset. Suddenly my heart is saying, "Let's do this! It's not about me anyway! It's Christ coming through me!" Scripture tells us that the robe of Christ's righteousness has been put on you and me; that when God sees us, He sees us through Christ and He says, "When I look at you, all I can see is the righteousness of Christ. There's no more shame. There's only Christ."

As we daily receive that covering, and say, "I'm Christ in Nick Stumbo," or "I'm Christ in _____" (fill in the blank with your name), there's a sudden confidence and a courage to risk. We gain a courage to go into places where we might feel weak, vulnerable or exposed, but we're able to say, "It's not just me, it's Christ in me."

Friends, even on your worst day, you can live encouraged; you can face the truth. You can be a community of grace because you have been covered by the righteousness of Jesus Christ. No matter what you've been through, no matter what's been done to you, no matter what you've done to others, the covering of Christ is yours. Through Jesus Christ, God says to you, "I've got you covered, kid." We can rise up in courage and in faith because of that covering.

CHAPTER 5
PEOPLE OF GRACE

James was the brother of Jesus and he wrote a short letter to encourage believers throughout Asia Minor. These are his words, starting in James 5:13:

> *"Are any of you suffering hardships? (To which we would say, "Yes"). You should pray. Are any of you happy? You should sing praises. Are any of you sick? You should call for the elders of the church to come and pray over you, anointing you with oil in the name of the Lord. Such a prayer offered in faith will heal the sick, and the Lord will make you well. And, if you committed any sins, you will be forgiven. Confess your sins to each other and pray for each other, so that you may be healed. The earnest prayer of a righteous person has great power and produces wonderful results."*[36]

There are a lot of words in this passage—a lot of phrases—that probably strike you as being attractive and appealing. The power of prayer producing wonderful results. Who doesn't want that?

---

36. James 5:13-16

I'm game. I'll take some powerful prayer, producing wonderful results! In this passage, James says to sing praises, call for the elders, anoint the sick. Great! I would take it all.

But, as you read through this passage, doesn't one phrase feel a little different? Doesn't one particular word cause a different emotion to come up inside your soul? The word I'm referring to, and maybe you've already guessed it, is "confess." How does *that* word make you feel?

CONFESS

Think about that word. What rises up in you when you hear the word *confess*? Maybe you respond by thinking, *I've been caught in something, and now I'm being told to confess the whole story.* We might feel like we're being interrogated, put on the spot, humiliated, or exposed. Confess. Who would want to confess? Criminals confess. Five-year-olds with cookie crumbs on their cheek confess. If we're honest, most of us have a somewhat negative—even visceral—reaction to the word *confess*. We may feel walls go up and emotional doors close. *You can't make me confess. Why would I want to do that?*

Yet, James highlights the incredible power of confession. *Confess...and you will be healed.* As we have been walking through this idea of becoming safe and creating a culture of grace, I hope that you've been challenged by the ideas so far. The thrust of this book thus far has been to live in the light. Let Jesus truly see you (Zacchaeus), find grace through absolute truth (the woman caught in adultery), and come out of hiding (Adam and Eve). But in all of these concepts, there is a great risk, is there not? A risk to confess. A risk to be open. A risk to get on the outside what

CHAPTER 5: PEOPLE OF GRACE

I've been keeping on the inside. Choosing to make my stuff—my secret thoughts and behaviors—plain and known to others can be intimidating. That's the risk: to dare to be known as a sinner.

I want to be upfront and tell you that my goal, by the end of this chapter, is that you might find yourself desiring to engage regularly in confession. Can I do it? Can we get there together? I have no idea, but let's at least attempt it, because James is saying something pretty profound.

James says that if you confess your sins and pray for one another you will be healed. I want to point out that the language here isn't chronological. James isn't giving an order of events, saying that if you will first confess and get all the bad stuff out of the way, then second, you'll be good enough to be worthy of healing. That's not what he's saying. If you look at the Greek language, these verbs are actually in a tense that we don't tend to think about, but use quite often in English. It's called the "imperfect tense," which means these words imply a continuous action. A better way to read this might be, "In *confessing* your sins and *praying* for one another, you will be healed."

James is actually saying that confessing is part of the healing. How could that be? Why is it that confessing—getting on the outside what we've been keeping on the inside—and having others pray for us, would be the context of the healing; not just the preamble to get out of the way so that we can be healed? James is saying that as you're confessing and as you're praying, God will bring healing. Well, if that's the case, maybe confessing is an activity you and I ought to desire more often.

So how can I find the courage and the desire to confess? It does take courage. It's a risk. It's putting something out there when you're not sure how people will react. Confessing will take some courage. Where will that courage come from? In order to answer that question, let's look together at another passage in Luke.

Luke 15:1 says, *"The tax collectors and other notorious sinners often came to listen to Jesus teach."* Here's another example in the Gospel where people who are nothing like Jesus, liked Jesus. Though they were very far from Him in their behaviors, lifestyle and their way of thinking, they liked to be around Jesus. In this passage, we find the "sinful" crowd flocking to Jesus and it's creating a reaction.

"This made the Pharisees and teachers of religious law complain that he was associating with such sinful people; even eating with them."[37] To us, that might not seem like such a big deal. We eat with all kinds of people in many different environments; but if you remember from the story of Zacchaeus in chapter 2, to share a meal with someone was to embrace them. Eating together meant to be identified with them. Jesus did this regularly and He drove the religious elites crazy with this behavior.

The truth is, they wanted Jesus to be like them, but Jesus didn't really seem that interested in trying to be like them. His association with the outcasts of their religious society made the Pharisees so angry that they couldn't have any grace for these people coming to Jesus.

In response to them, Jesus tells three stories. These may be familiar stories to you. He tells a story about a lost sheep, a lost coin, and then in verse 11, a story about a lost son. The three stories all make the same point. Why three stories? Jesus knew that His main point would be a big change in their thinking, so He approached it from three different angles. But, He definitely saved the best for last.

---

37. Luke 15:2

CHAPTER 5: PEOPLE OF GRACE

This is where we will pick up the story. *"To illustrate his point further, Jesus told them this story: a man had two sons. The younger son told his father, 'I want my share of your estate now before you die.'"*[38]

In Jesus' day, sons always received an inheritance from their father—when Dad died! The younger son is essentially saying, "Dad, I hope you die, but because you won't die, I'd like my money now. It's as if you were dead. Give me my money so that I can do with it what I want now." Such a request would have been unheard of for the crowd. This is what makes the father's response in the story so surprising: *"So his father agreed to divide his wealth between his sons. A few days later this younger son packed all his belongings and moved to a distant land, and there he wasted all his money in wild living. About the time his money ran out, a great famine swept over the land and he began to starve. He persuaded a local farmer to hire him, and the man sent him into his fields to feed the pigs. The young man became so hungry that even the pods that he was feeding the pigs looked good to him. But, no one gave him anything."*[39]

At this point in the story, all the mouths in the Jewish audience would have dropped open. This would have been rock bottom for a Jewish young man to be out feeding the animals that, in their religion, were filthy and dirty and not to be associated with. But, this is where the young man is. He's in the pigpen, and the food there looks pretty good.

---

38. Luke 15:11-12
39. Luke 15:12-16

THE MEANING OF LOST

I want to take a moment and be very clear about what it means to be lost in this passage. Jesus says the son was lost. In modern terminology one way that we talk about lost, especially in church, means someone who has rejected faith in Christ, or they have never heard the message at all. So in this sense, they are "lost" from God. This is a modern construct of the word that would have been foreign to Jesus' audience that day. They were a Jewish crowd listening to a Jewish teacher tell a story that, in their minds, was about a Jewish young man and a Jewish father. It was all in the context of Jewishness; people within the same community. He wasn't lost in the sense that he didn't know God or didn't know the truth.

It's also not the same sense of lost which Jesus refers to in the previous story about a coin. In this story, a woman lost a coin; like, "Oops, I dropped a coin. I can't find it. It's lost." The son's "lost" isn't incidental or an accident. No, this *lost* was the son's own doing. It was his choice to get lost; to take his father's money, move far away, waste it all and end up destitute and desperate. Jesus was telling a story about an incredibly offensive son who says, "Dad, I reject your authority over me, I reject your home and your name, and all the covering you can give me. I'm going to strike out on my own because I don't want what you can offer me." That's what Jesus is referring to as a lost son. He had gotten himself lost.

As we think about where we might find our place in this story, this is key to our understanding. Our "lost-ness" is our doing. In any area of our life where we find ourselves separated or distant from what we thought we should be doing, or from what God had called us to do, we need to acknowledge that we have made some decisions. I have taken some steps to get myself to this lost place. We don't just think of it as accidental, "Oops, how did I get here?" Instead, we are willing to honestly look back at the choices we made.

Does this mean that everything is our fault? No. Does this mean that no one else had a role to play in the story? Absolutely not. Others may have had a significant role in hurting, abusing, or shaming us to the point where we wanted to run. But even in extreme cases of abuse, we make choices to isolate, hide or run from God and others who are able to help us. In one way or another, we have all chosen a path of isolation.

This illustration can help us see this path:

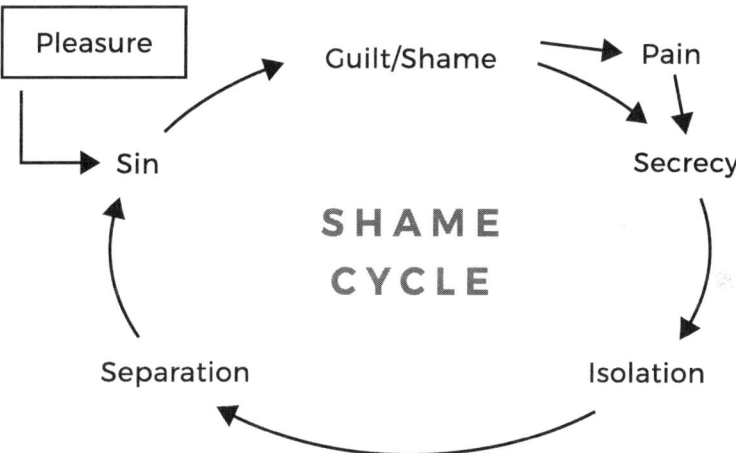

Here's what happens in this cycle. The young man starts in the same place where all of us start at one time or another. He desires *pleasure*. Whether you like that word or not—maybe you prefer the word happiness, joy or well-being—we have a brain that is wired to desire pleasure. We are pleasure-seekers. Sometimes that pursuit of pleasure will lead us into bad choices or wrong behavior, and we might call that *sin*.

So, the young man, desiring pleasure, runs off and spends all his money in wild living. When we live separate from God or from our own sense of what's right and wrong, it produces *guilt*. As we previously discussed, guilt says I did something bad and can morph into something even more dangerous, which is *shame*. Shame says I am bad. Whether we're feeling like I did something bad or I am bad, these are feelings that in our mind, and in our heart, we have to deal with.

What we choose to do—as I believe the young man did in the story—is make a decision to *hide*. Maybe not physical hiding, like Adam and Eve, but we hide emotionally or relationally. We feel the need to act like things are okay; we decide to power up and make it through. We hide the things that we feel others don't need to know. The danger is that the moment we begin to hide, it leads us to another place that maybe we didn't really mean to choose, but it happens because we're hiding. We find ourselves in *isolation*.

The moment we have something to hide, we can't help but begin to isolate from others around us. There's a small part of us, or maybe a big piece of us, that they don't know. This creates a barrier, a gap between us and other people. The real danger in isolation is we don't just stay there; if you begin to isolate internally, it bleeds into another step that we might not feel we are consciously choosing. When we remain in isolation and don't deal with it, we are choosing *separation*. Isolation, internally, will always lead us to separation relationally—space between us, others and God, where we end up alone.

Do you see this in the young man's story? He was off feeding the pigs, and the food looked good to him. But what was the last phrase we saw in Luke 15? *No one gave him anything*; which is another way of saying he had completely separated himself from people who cared, from the people who knew what he needed.

CHAPTER 5: PEOPLE OF GRACE

In his place of deep desperation, nobody was there to help. His hiding had caused isolation which led to separation. He was alone. This all began from seeking pleasure; leading him into sin and taking him down this path.

What's scary about this system, the *Shame Cycle*,[40] is that it has a way of self-perpetuating. When we live in places of separation from God and others, it becomes much easier to choose sin. As we choose sin, we experience an ever-increasing level of guilt or shame, which makes us feel like we have even more to hide. The more we hide, the more isolated we feel. The more isolated we feel, the more separated we become. This cycle just keeps on going. It repeats over and over and over in a downward spiral.

If we continue in it long enough, our sin no longer produces guilt or shame; we become numb to it. Our brain begins to disengage emotionally, socially, and spiritually as a way of coping with our own behavior. A person who has become numb to their own behavior is doomed to repeat it. Is there a way out? You better believe it.

When we get caught in the spin cycle of shame, or hit rock bottom, we can feel it. Sometimes, our reaction is to try and better ourselves by shutting off all pleasure. "I will never seek pleasure again. I don't need any of it in my life." Well, good luck with that. As I said, your brain is wired to be a pleasure-seeking brain. It longs for joy. Stopping our pursuit of pleasure doesn't work.

Others have said, "Yeah, I can't stop pleasure, but I'll never sin again. I will never, ever, ever, ever, ever, do this again. Well, maybe this one last time; and then after this one last time, I will never

---

40. Roberts, T. (2009). *Seven Pillars of Freedom Workbook*. Gresham, OR: Pure Desire Ministries International.

ever…Okay one more time, but then after that, never ever…maybe one more." You see what I'm getting at? As human beings, sooner or later, we're going to find ourselves in sin again. The answer is not found in trying to eliminate pleasure or to avoid all sin, and trying to be perfect for the rest of our lives. The solution lies elsewhere.

A DIFFERENT PATH

Let's return to our story and see what the young man does. This is a great sentence; take a look at this. *"When he finally came to his senses…"*[41]

The original Greek wording here says, "He finally came to himself." He faced himself and the honest truth of his situation. He became aware of his reality, *"…and he said to himself, 'At home, even the hired servants have food enough to spare, and here I am dying of hunger. I will go to my father and I will say, 'Father, I have sinned against both heaven and you, and I am no longer worthy of being called your son. Please take me on as a hired servant.' So he returned home to his father."*[42]

In coming to himself—in facing the truth of his situation—the son came to a place of repentance. It took him in a different direction on this cycle. If we go back to our illustration, our feelings of guilt and shame are actually a crossroad. We can go in one of two directions. We can ignore the pain of honesty and hide, which sends us spiraling into isolation, or we can choose something different. The word I would use, simply put, is honesty. Being honest is a choice to face the pain. Please notice: he wasn't

---

41. Luke 15:17
42. Luke 15:17-20

being honest with anyone else at this point except himself. He was simply saying to himself, "I'm stuck and I can't rescue myself."

Honesty begins when we admit we can't rescue ourselves. We realize that we are in a place of isolation and separation, and trying harder simply will not work. If I try harder to work my way out of it, by myself, I will only perpetuate a cycle of aloneness, and I will stay separated.

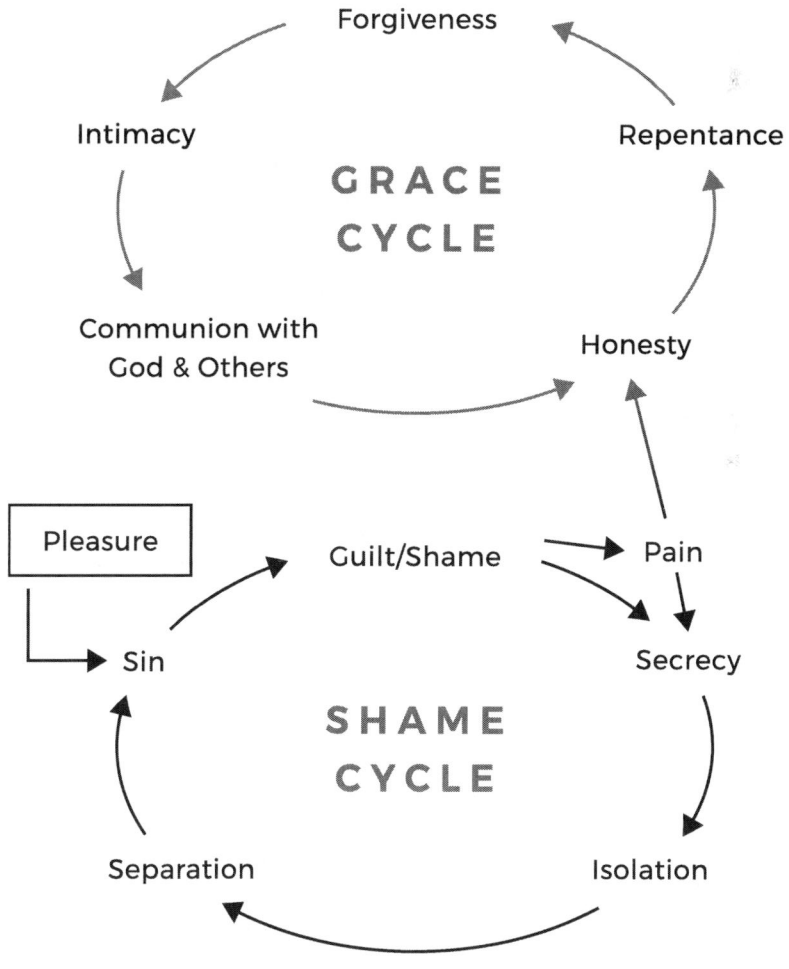

Breaking out of the *Shame Cycle* always requires an honest moment with yourself to say, "I'm stuck. I got here by myself. I'm not going to fix it by myself." The sickness and the cure can't come from the same medicine. Self-effort and isolation got us into our mess; we can't crawl back into that same cave and hope to be made well.

In that place of honesty, the lost son realizes what we all must realize, "I need others." He thinks of his father back home and makes a bargain with himself when he realizes, "My dad's slaves are better off than I am. Certainly, I could be one of them." And he heads home.

> *"So he returned home to his father. And while he was still a long way off, his father saw him coming. Filled with love and compassion, he ran to his son, embraced him, and kissed him. His son said to him,* (he's got a speech all ready to go) *'Father, I have sinned against both heaven and you, and I am no longer worthy of being called your son.'"*[43]

Do you see how deep the son's sense of worthlessness runs? In his confession, he's saying, "I'm not even worthy of being called your son." Isolation and separation has this devastating effect on all of us. In the absence of true voices speaking God's worth into us, we buy into a lie that we are no longer worthy. The lost son is explaining and bemoaning his own worthlessness. But do you see what he's missing? He has overlooked the incredible actions his father has already taken on his behalf.

In this story, the Jewish father has just done two things that would have completely shocked every father in Jesus' first century audience. Jewish men did not run. It's not like our culture where

---

43. Luke 15:20-21

CHAPTER 5: PEOPLE OF GRACE

grown men can do crazy things like run ultra-marathons. They didn't do that in the first century, especially wealthy men, who owned estates and land. They wore long robes. They had slaves to fetch whatever they needed.

The other thing Jewish men did not do was show physical compassion to other men, much less to a wayward son who had wished them dead! But this father, filled with such compassion, runs to his son, embraces him, and kisses him. The son is so filled with his own lies of worthlessness that he misses all of his father's compassion. His driving sense of worthlessness blinds him to the father's incredible love.

I bring up this point because I wonder how many people—how many of us sitting in church every weekend—are so stuck in a cycle of shame that we can't see a Father who is loving us with a compassion and grace like we've never experienced before. It's going right over our head because of the lies of shame and isolation.

We should pause and ask ourselves an important question: Do we believe that God is safe? Not safe as in "tame and predictable," but safe in a way that He can be trusted with the worst of who we are. We might say God is safe, but unless we feel like running to Him on our worst days and at our worst moments, we have projected onto God an image, a false image, that is not safe. The image of the father in the prodigal son story helps us see God as He truly is—safe. His grace is great enough to look through our stuff to see our true identity.

Next, the son takes a very important step down a new path. His honesty leads to something very important. It leads him to confession; to openly acknowledge what had gone wrong. He got on the outside what was happening on the inside, saying, "Father, I've blown it." He takes the risk. He dares to be a sinner. He dares to admit, "I don't feel worthy. Here it is. What now?"

Look what the father does as the son is repeating his little speech. Before he can even finish it, the father interrupts him, "*But his father said to the servants, 'Quick! Bring the finest robe in the house, and put it on him, and bring a ring for his finger and sandals for his feet.*"[44]

All of these, by the way, would have identified him as a son: putting the father's name and identity over his shoulders and on his hands and on his feet, so that when people saw him—even from a mile away—they recognize he is a son. He belongs. He's a part of the family. Bring all those things, and by the way, kill that calf that we've been fattening for a holiday meal. Get to work on the T-bone steaks. "*We must celebrate with a feast, for this son of mine was dead and now has returned to life. He was lost, but now he is found. So the party began.*"[45]

Don't you love it? So the party began! This young man faced his worst fears in coming home. He risked honesty, fully expecting an angry father to sentence him to hard labor in the fields. But instead, the father lavishes love and compassion on him far beyond what he could have ever imagined! This party was all about bestowing on this lost son identity, belonging and value, returning him fully to a place of sonship. Wow!

What I want you to see is this connection. Because the son made the move for honesty and confession, because he dared to take the risk to be a sinner, that's what enabled him to experience forgiveness. The father is able to say, "It's okay, I love you," because the son was willing to confess. This brought *forgiveness*, and forgiveness led to something even better: *intimacy*.

---

44. Luke 15:22
45. Luke 15:23-24

CHAPTER 5: PEOPLE OF GRACE

I know, some of you just got very uncomfortable. You read that word and images or ideas flash into your head. In our sex-saturated culture, we've made intimacy synonymous with sex. Can we take a moment and redeem that word? Intimacy does not mean sex. Intimacy is a word that means being truthful, vulnerable, and known, and still loved. It's a deep knowledge of another person and complete acceptance of them. It's why the biblical word for sex in the Greek and Hebrew language was the word closest to knowledge; *knowing* another person.

Intimacy is trust and vulnerability in real openness. It's the kind of relationship God intended for you and me to have with Him; not based on our sexuality, but based on vulnerability. There's nothing being hidden and no isolation. In honesty and confession, we are able to say, "This is who I am," and in that place experiencing forgiveness. Forgiveness and intimacy lead us to the kind of relationships we are meant to have: *communion* with God and others.

Look back at the chart for a minute: at a place of guilt and shame, the lost son chose honesty. He was honest with himself and God. This brought him to risk confession. He opened up to his father, and because he was open, his father was able to offer forgiveness, which created new intimacy between them. Intimacy with the father created communion with God and others.

Do you know the best part? Just like the *Shame Cycle* is a continuing, self-perpetuating path, so is the *Grace Cycle*. As we choose to engage in relationship with God and others, this creates a greater openness on our part to confession. We continue along the path of intimacy, and the more we have, the more pleasurable it becomes. Rather than choosing sin, we begin to choose relationships because of the joy they bring. This can happen for you!

WHAT ABOUT THAT OTHER GUY?

The lost son has come home. He expected a sentence and received a party instead. Well, Amen and Hallelujah! Close the book. Great story. Let's pray, right? But, there were how many sons in the story? Two sons. Not a trick question. Two sons, and we met the younger. Now let's meet the older.

> *"Meanwhile, the older son was in the fields working. When he returned home, he heard music and dancing in the house and he asked one of the servants what was going on. 'Your brother is back,' he was told, 'and your father has killed the fattened calf. We are celebrating because of his safe return.' The older brother was angry and wouldn't go in. His father came out and begged him, but he replied, 'All these years, I've slaved for you and never once refused to do a single thing you told me to. And in all that time you never gave me even one young goat for a feast with my friends. Yet when this son of yours comes back after squandering your money on prostitutes, you celebrate by killing the fattened calf."*[46]

As we deal with confession, we must beware of the spirit of the older brother, especially if we've grown up in church. For us, growing up in church and trying to do the right thing is the equivalent of saying, "I've been in the fields working. I've been doing the right things. I've been toeing the line. I know I'm not perfect, but for the most part, God, I've done what you told me to do." When someone else comes along and admits to totally blowing it, we might be irritated that God would you give them so much grace!

---

46. Luke 15:25-30

CHAPTER 5: PEOPLE OF GRACE

But this brings us to Jesus' entire reason for telling the story. Jesus is speaking to the religious elites; He is making a parallel between them and the older brother. Jesus is communicating a message that says, "When the younger brother, who's been lost, comes back and acknowledges his sin and finds forgiveness, that's the time to throw the party. Not the time to throw in the towel. It's not time to look them over and write them off. It's time to embrace them, invite them in and celebrate a new beginning." The older brother refused the father's invitation to the party, and in doing so, showed he had missed the meaning of grace.

The elder brother missed out. Why? Because he couldn't stand the unmerited grace of the father, especially when he felt left out. Someone else was being treated with grace that they didn't deserve, and he couldn't stand it because he believed he deserved so much. But, the father said to him, *"Look, dear son, you have always stayed by me and everything I have is yours. We had to celebrate this happy day. For your brother was dead and has come back to life! He was lost, but now he is found."*[47]

In one phrase, the father puts our whole illustration into perspective. He says clearly, "This *Shame Cycle* is what it means to be lost, and this *Grace Cycle* is what it means to be found." The younger son was dead—he was separated, isolated and alone, but now he's alive—he has found forgiveness, intimacy and communion with others; so there's a party. If you're willing, you can join.

This is what it looks like to be a culture of grace. This is the power that confession can have in a community of people. Simply put, confession is the currency that transfers us from sickness to health. Confession is the pathway that breaks us out of the cycle of

---

47. Luke 15:31-32

sickness, being lost, and death. It puts us on a new path of health, being found, and experiencing life.

That's why James can say (in James 5) that in confessing to one another, and praying for one another, you will experience healing. It is the confessing that puts you on the path of life.

From only a few of the dozens of passages that could be quoted, consider the record of Scripture:

> *People who conceal their sins will not prosper, but if they confess and turn from them they will receive mercy.*
> PROVERBS 28:13

> *When I refused to confess my sin, my body wasted away, and I groaned all day long. Day and night your hand of discipline was heavy on me. My strength evaporated like water in the summer heat. Finally, I confessed all my sins to you and stopped trying to hide my guilt. I said to myself, "I will confess my rebellion to the LORD."*
> *And you forgave me and all my guilt is gone.*
> PSALM 32:3-5

> *But if we confess our sins to him, he is faithful and just to forgive us our sins and to cleanse us from all wickedness.*
> I JOHN 1:9

Confession is the currency that transfers us into the account of God's grace!

WHAT ABOUT A CULTURE OF GRACE?

You might be thinking by now, "Nick, I thought we were going to talk about becoming a culture of grace, but you keep telling me

CHAPTER 5: PEOPLE OF GRACE

about things that I need to do as an individual, and something hard to do at that! Couldn't we just talk about being nicer to one another at church or being more accepting as a community?" We could, but the reality is that the more people in a culture who consistently live out a *Grace Cycle*, the more that culture will be marked by grace.

If we simply focus as a group of people—as a church, small group, or family—on being nicer to each other or more accepting of one another, we can do all of that and still be stuck in a *Shame Cycle*: separated and isolated from one another. If we merely try to be nicer to one another but haven't dealt with our shame and what is hidden, we'll just be smiling a little more than we were before. Maybe we shake a few more hands and offer an extra kind hello, but this elevated niceness doesn't change anyone. In fact, if anything, it pushes us deeper into shame; we become convinced that all the smiling, hand-shaking people are holy and we are not.

But the more of us who live out a *Grace Cycle*, where we have found that it's okay to be real—to have sin in our lives—the more we create that same culture around us. When we confess in order to experience the incredible healing that comes through forgiveness and intimacy with God and others, it has a powerful way of inviting a whole community into the party. Isn't that a place you would like to be a part of? I know I would!

So, how does this happen? Let me give you four ways we can move toward confession and take the path of grace.

1. DARE TO BE A SINNER.

By this, I don't mean that we should go out and sin more. We're pretty good at that on our own. You don't need me or anyone else to encourage that! I also don't mean that we should be flippant about our sinfulness and brag of things we have done. Instead, what I mean is that we must dare to be honest about the real us. No more hiding. In those places where sin is happening and where we're broken, we must choose to reveal the truth.

The reality of this lost-and-found cycle is that you don't have to be stuck in the lost cycle in every area of your life. You only need to be stuck in the lost cycle in one area. If, even in one area of life, we feel the need to hide, that one area alone is creating isolation. If it's creating isolation, it will lead us to separation, and it will be self-perpetuating. If we're stuck there, even in one place, we're stuck. So, dare to be a sinner.

The fact that we're not blatant prodigals—rebelling from God or others in every area of our life—is what keeps us in hiding and isolation. For the most part, we see ourselves as "pretty good." So that one area, that outlier, feels so incongruous that the temptation to hide it can be insurmountable. But we must not hide it! Dietrich Bonhoeffer put the challenge this way:

> He who is alone with his sin is utterly alone. It may be that Christians, notwithstanding corporate worship, common prayer, and all their fellowship in service, may still be left to their loneliness. The final break-through to fellowship does not occur, because, though they have fellowship with one another as believers and as devout people, they do not have fellowship as the undevout, as sinners. The pious fellowship permits no one to be a sinner. So everybody must conceal his sin from himself and from the fellowship. We dare not be sinners. Many Christians are unthinkably horrified when a real sinner is suddenly discovered among the righteous. So we remain alone with our sin, living in lies and hypocrisy. The fact is that we are sinners.[48]

48. Bonhoeffer, D. (1954). *Life Together: The Classic Exploration of Christian in Community.* New York, NY: Harper & Row Publishers, Inc.

CHAPTER 5: PEOPLE OF GRACE

We are sinners! We all know this, yet somehow we think it is our righteous facade that provides acceptance from others. If we all could let down our guard and dare to be sinners, we would find a form of communion, and community, we desperately long for.

At a national gathering of pastors, I had the privilege of hearing Joni Erickson Tada share about her life. You may know her story, but if you don't, she has been a quadriplegic for almost 50 years. Through her journey with this condition, God has given her a ministry: a writing, speaking, music, and camp ministry. She has a tremendous influence around the world. Here is this woman who's been in a wheelchair for over 50 years and in this particular talk she said, "God has used my condition to continually reveal to me what a dog-nasty sinner I am."[49]

As I looked at this sixty-something-year-old woman, my opinion was that she must be one of the most humble, polite, and gracious women I have ever seen. But if she can think of herself as a "dog-nasty" sinner, who am I to be so self-righteous?

She was revealing that it's not about what we do with our hands as much as what's going on in our hearts—in our minds— and she was willing to acknowledge that she was a sinner in need of grace every day. Her talk that day convinced me that if she can say that about herself, I can too.

Dare to be a sinner, because in doing so we enter into a place of confession and forgiveness.

---

49. The Christian and Missionary Alliance National Council (2015). Guest Speaker: Joni Erickson Tada. Long Beach, CA.

2. GUARD AGAINST A CLEANED-UP CONFESSION.

Some of us might get the idea that, yes, confession is good; so we are going to go to someone and finally get on the outside what we've been holding on the inside. Yet, even as we start to confess, we'll feel this temptation to try and look good. We're going to leave out the details that make it particularly incriminating or leave us feeling especially guilty. We're going to try to sound decent even in confession.

Don't do that. In fact, it's one of the reasons why, when guys come to a group and start their journey toward sexual purity, one of the first things I tell them is, "Don't go home and spill it all to your wife." In light of this chapter on confession, that statement might not make any sense, so allow me to explain.

The image I use is of vomiting—confessing our stuff is a little like throwing up. Anytime we throw up, we feel better, but the recipient of our vomit feels awful! The real danger here is that for a guy coming out of addiction, there's more to come! We so easily get caught up in a system of lying to ourselves and others that we aren't able to fully and honestly expose what needs exposing. We clean up our confession. A confession—a full, thought-out thorough confession—will happen as part of the process. But the pain of staggered disclosure, where the truth comes out bit by bit, is the traumatic equivalent to that of a rape victim.[50]

Right now, this would be my encouragement to you as you think about how to enter into honesty and confession. Find a brother or a sister in Christ who you do not owe a confession.

---

[50] Corely, D. & Schneider, J. (2012). *Disclosing Secrets: An Addict's Guide for When, to Whom, & How Much to Reveal.* Wickenburg, AZ; Gentle Path Press.

CHAPTER 5: PEOPLE OF GRACE

(Meaning, your offense or sin is not against them.) Find someone that you can go to and tell exactly where you are stuck. Encourage them to ask questions and clarify the full story. Find someone who won't let you sugar-coat it, dance around the edges, or speak in vague generalities. Demand of yourself a rugged truthfulness, and as you do, that self-deceit will begin to dissipate. You'll begin to see yourself clearly and you will soon be able to go to the person to whom you have wronged, whether it's a spouse or family member, and truly confess in a right way without cleaning it up to look better.

3. FIND FATHERS, NOT OLDER BROTHERS.

Find people that you believe might respond to you as the father did with grace, compassion, humility and joy. A father who will say, "I'm so glad you've come. Let's talk. I love you." Try to avoid the older brothers that will say, "It's about time. Clean up your act and get it together, would ya?" We must find fathers, because if we only confess to God, then we will stay stuck in the cycle of aloneness. When we confess only to God, as Bonhoeffer said, we may find that we're only confessing to ourselves and granting ourselves forgiveness!

Self-forgiveness has no power to change us. It can be helpful and healthy, but we can also deceive ourselves and justify anything. But, in confessing to another, the veil of self-deceit is removed. I can see myself clearly, and I can receive the forgiveness of God through the presence of another. So find fathers, not older brothers.

4. BE WILLING TO BE A FATHER, NOT AN OLDER BROTHER.

Here's the catch: if we want to have fathers to confess to, we must also learn to be a father to others. If we're going to be a safe person, when someone comes to us and says, "I've really blown it!" we've got to be like the father and give compassion. This moment has a beauty in it that should be celebrated. A heart, a prodigal heart, has made the move to turn back toward God and community through repentance. Our reaction needs to be one of affirmation and celebration. We are the one to welcome them home.

One truly amazing aspect of our faith in Christ is that He actually says you and I have the power to mete out the forgiveness of God. Let that sink in for a moment. Jesus puts the keys to God's grace in our hands:

> *Then He breathed on them and said, "Receive the Holy Spirit. If you forgive anyone's sins, they are forgiven. If you do not forgive them, they are not forgiven."*[51]

You and I have the power to forgive someone else in the name of Jesus. When you forgive them, it's like Jesus forgave them. Have you ever thought about that? You can say to a friend in Christ, "In the name of Jesus, I forgive you," and it's as if Jesus Himself was forgiving them. Wow! That's a power that could change the world, one culture a time. So be the father and not the older brother when someone confesses to you. Offer grace and not the try-harder-next-time condemnation.

What if you are in an environment where it isn't safe to confess? Some groups or people can be so trapped in a rule-bound, grace-less culture that they are unable to receive the open confession of others. The spirit of the older brother can quickly shame a person who is attempting to walk in confession!

As I encourage you toward confession, I am making such assumptions. I am assuming that you are in a position of culture-

---

51. John 20:22-23 NIV

CHAPTER 5: PEOPLE OF GRACE

creating; either as a leader in your church or small group, or a leader in your home (parent, spouse, grandparent). If you are in a position of culture-creating, you can always set the tone by your vulnerability and openness. You can make it a safe place to confess. My other assumption is that you are in a culture where confession would be welcomed!

But what if you are in a position where you are not part of culture-creating, such as a member of the congregation or a child in the home? Or what if your culture or environment isn't safe for honesty? In this case, you need to discern where it IS safe to confess. If you don't know if the leadership in your church would be safe to confess to, perhaps you could go first to a trusted friend. If your parents or authority in the home have consistently shamed anyone who admits faults, maybe you would find a group outside the home where confession is welcomed. If your fear of confession is rooted in a track-record of shaming and condemning of those who confess, you are wise to seek out another safe place where you might find the attitude of the father from Luke 15.

As James, the brother of Jesus, said: As we are confessing, and as we are praying with each other, we will experience healing. And we will be a culture of grace.

Did I make you desire confession a little bit? I hope so. Confession opens the door to life in communion with God and others. That is a party we don't want to miss!

Confession is where it begins moving us down the path to deep, abiding relationships with God and others. The key word in that sentence is *begins*. Too often, we think of confession as an *end* in and of itself. Confession, however, is not the end goal of faith. Confession opens the door. To what, you may ask? That's what we'll look at in our next chapter.

CHAPTER 6
DO UNTO OTHERS

I love to work in my lawn. In particular, I love to mow my lawn. I'll even mow my lawn when it doesn't need it. The task has a clear beginning and end. When I'm finished, I can look back and see that something has been accomplished. What was at first an uneven, chaotic carpet of green shoots and weeds has been transformed into a nice, evenly-lined, well-manicured lawn. Walking behind the mower on a sunny Saturday afternoon is a sort of therapy for me.

On one occasion, though, my task of lawn mowing didn't go so well. Foolishly, I chose to engage in hand-to-hand combat with my lawn mower; not something I would recommend.

Now, you need to know something about my lawn mower. Lawn mowers, in general, have a bar that you hold down. When this is done, you engage the engine so you can start it up. As soon as you let go of this bar, the engine stops. On my machine, that mechanism—a well-designed safety mechanism, mind you—had broken. Not a problem, as I found a way to bypass the system by rigging the engine to always be in the "on" position. Unfortunately, you can always find a way to out-stupid a safety feature if you really try! This meant that when I stopped mowing and needed to empty the bag, the mower would still be running. You can see this recipe for disaster coming, can't you?

You need to know something else about my family story. About seven or eight years ago, an uncle of mine had also chosen to do hand-to-hand combat with his mower. This Stumbo relative actually lost a portion of one of his digits in the battle. He went into the emergency room for treatment, and as he waited a doctor came in. According to my uncle's story, this doctor did nothing but look at his chart and tell jokes using his last name, Stumbo. The doctor jested that he was now a "Stump"-bo. I'm not kidding you. From then on, he was known as Stump-bo by the emergency room's staff.

I tell you that story because every time I go to start my lawn mower, and I mean every time, I jokingly think to myself, "Okay, don't be a Stump-bo today!" So, with those pieces of information in mind, here's my story. My lawn was really long and I was trying to mow it particularly short in preparation for winter. It didn't take long for the bag to get full and start clogging with grass clippings. As I removed the bag—remember, with the engine still running and the blade still spinning—I saw a big chunk of grass down by the catcher. So I thought, "I'm just going to grab that and get it in the bag." You're probably cringing now because you know what comes next—I grabbed a little too close to the spinning blade and ka-thunk! The blade hit my hand.

At that moment, the first thought that went through my mind was, "Oh no! I just did a Stump-bo!" I looked down at my hand and feared the worst. But thank God for good leather gloves and dull mower blades, because I didn't do any more damage than deeply bruising my fingers and my ego. It took several months for my hand to feel normal again, but it could have been far, far worse. This was not my best decision.

CHAPTER 6: DO UNTO OTHERS

Now, as you read this story, you may have one of two reactions. On the one hand, you might be thinking, "Okay, you disabled the safety feature and you have a story in your family where a similar thing happened. Sounds like you got exactly what you deserved. You were asking for this, pal!" Or, on the other hand, if you're a little more kind-hearted, you might find yourself thinking, "Friend, this could have been so much worse for you! I mean, you could have been in the emergency room and had permanent damage. You were so fortunate to NOT get what you deserved."

Either way you react to this story, it makes me think about "getting what we deserve." When it comes to this idea of grace, we might use this phrase as part of our definition of the word. Grace is either getting something we don't deserve, like an undeserved gift, or it's not getting something that we do deserve, like an undeserved reprieve. It's having mercy when we don't get some kind of punishment.

Is that what grace is all about? In fact, Jesus said something similar to that in His Sermon on the Mount.[52] He said that we should do unto others as we would have them do unto us. Great statement. Great principle to practice in your life. How should I treat this person? How would I want them to treat me? A lot of truth there.

But I would argue that Jesus didn't intend to make this a statement about grace. His principle comes short of capturing the picture of grace that God has for us. The problem with that statement, "What do you deserve or what do I deserve," is that the foundation of grace is still "me." Right? It's asking, "What do I deserve and then give that to others. What do they deserve?" I try

---

52. Matthew 7:12

to be kind to them based on what I deem kindness to be. This is an insufficient foundation because I am still the standard of what type of grace should be given or received.

I want to look at a picture from God's Word of a much more robust and fuller definition of grace; a definition that I think is enough to lead us into the future.

In this book, we've been asking this question: How could we become a culture of grace? We've looked at how people in the Bible—people in the first century—that were nothing like Jesus, liked Jesus. They were the outcasts, the notorious sinners, the people that everyone else had slammed the door on and turned away. They loved Jesus; not because Jesus taught some really lame, watered-down theology. No. If anything, Jesus taught harder things for them. He said, *"You have heard the commandment that says, 'You must not commit adultery.' But I say, anyone who even looks at a woman with lust has already committed adultery with her in his heart."*[53] Everyone in the crowd would have said, "Wow! How can that be?" Even still, people that were known to be notorious sinners couldn't help but flock to Jesus.

We've asked the question, "How could we be a church where people, who are nothing like Jesus, like us because we're like Jesus?" I think it all comes down to this one word, "grace." How can we be people that are known for grace, and, more specifically, grace that goes beyond just giving or getting what we deserve?

We discover a powerful picture of grace in the Old Testament, in 2 Samuel 9. Let me give you some quick context for this chapter. King David reigns over Israel. David is only the second king that Israel has ever had, taking the place of King Saul. We know, both

---

53. Matthew 5:27-28

CHAPTER 6: DO UNTO OTHERS

biblically and historically, that the reign of King David was one of the most significant and powerful kingdoms in the entire world at that time.

By this time in 2 Samuel, David has established his throne, conquered Jerusalem, built his palace, and begun preparations for the temple. Chapter 8 starts off with the foreign nations he's conquered and defeated. Israel is experiencing peace in the land. Wealth. Riches. David has accomplished what a king sets out to do. So in 2 Samuel 9, we find David sitting on his throne asking himself the question, "Self, what should I do now? I've conquered our enemies, created order out of chaos. We're doing well! So what now?" And this is what comes to mind for David:

One day David asked, "Is anyone in Saul's family still alive..."

The crowd that first heard these words 3,000 years ago, when the king asked this question, would have had one very clear thought: he was looking for them to kill them. In that day and age, it was completely expected that when a new dynasty took over, they would look back to the previous dynasty and ask the question, "Does anyone else have a legitimate claim to my throne? Is there anyone else who could stir up the people and say, 'Hey, why is he the king? I've got the right bloodline. Make me king.'" Every person that hears King David speak this sentence is thinking the same thing: "Ah, he's going to take care of business, which he should. He is going to give them what they deserve! If they're of the former king's line, they must die. You can't have a new kingdom if the former kingdom is still around in competition."

This is exactly why David's next words are noteworthy. I cannot emphasize enough how bizarre this question would have been! David says,

> "Is anyone in Saul's family still alive—anyone to whom I can show kindness for Jonathan's sake? He summoned a man named Ziba who had been one of Saul's servants. "Are you Ziba?" the king asked. "Yes, sir. I am" Ziba replied. Then the king asked him, "Is anyone still alive from Saul's family? If so, I want to show kindness to them." Ziba replied, "Yes. One of Jonathan's sons is still alive. He is crippled in both feet." "Where is he?" the king asked. "In Lo Debar," Ziba told him, "at the home of Makir, son of Ammiel.""[54]

David's question, "Is there anyone to whom I can show kindness?" made no sense in this context. His desire to bless instead of curse, to protect a life rather than snuff it out, is the point of the passage.

But before we get to that, I want to point out a significant detail in this passage. The Scriptures are not written like a newspaper report. They aren't simply the factual reporting of what happened and why. The authors wrote with intent to communicate a message. The little details can help us see something. So, repetition is one verbal clue Old Testament authors would use to communicate significant details.

In this passage, four times we hear the name of Ziba. His name gets repeated to the point of being ridiculous. Are you Ziba? Yes, I'm Ziba. Ziba says. Ziba, Ziba, Ziba. Okay, we get it. His name is Ziba!

---

54. 2 Samuel 9:1-4

CHAPTER 6: DO UNTO OTHERS

Then, there is another guy. We know where he lives. It's a place called Lo Debar, which means "pasture-less." This might have been the literal name of this area or it might have been a way to say he lives in the middle of nowhere; far away.

We also know the name of the man he's staying with and the name of his father.

We get names all over the place, but when it comes to the person, who actually becomes the main character of this story, what identification does he get? A name? Nope.

Only this: *crippled in both feet.*

His identity, at this point, is "crippled in both feet." Ziba's name is everywhere; like it's going out of style. But this other fellow is named by his infirmity. He's a cripple, which would have made him an outcast.

Now, in truth, we know a little bit about his story from earlier in 2 Samuel. If we were reading through the whole book, in chapter 5 we would find a story about a boy named Mephibosheth. His story begins when he's only four or five years old according to the Scriptures. His story is a footnote in the tragic death of both King Saul and his son Jonathan in one battle.

When Mephibosheth's nursemaid hears about the death of the king and his son, she realizes the line of King Saul has come to an end. This puts Mephibosheth in grave danger. With both Saul and Jonathan gone, David's line is about to begin. Mephibosheth, being a surviving heir and the son of Jonathan himself, is going to be target number one. So, she scoops up this boy to flee Jerusalem for their lives. On their way out of town—we're not told exactly how it happens—she drops him. Perhaps, she stumbles and falls and he goes down some stairs. Whatever happens, he falls and breaks his feet so badly that he is crippled for life.

They run away to Lo Debar, to a pasture-less, faraway place. He's been dropped. A man crippled in both feet. This is not only his story, it is also his identity.

This brings me to the first principle of grace from this passage. The first principle is this: **Everyone has a story**.

Put another way: everyone has been dropped. We know this to be true, don't we? Everyone has a place in their life where something happened to them. An event or a story that occurred in their past or their background that has come to define them. It's not truly who they are, and yet, it has a way of becoming their perceived identity. They can live in its shadow all of their lives. We all can.

For you, perhaps the story is that you were the middle child, and the brother ahead of you was so good and so perfect, and the brother behind you was so loved and so special. And you, in the middle, felt like you were never enough. You felt you were never noticed, and you grew up with that awareness. You were dropped. It became part of your story. You may still battle against the emotions and triggers that make you feel left out or unheard. It's the pent-up frustration feeling like, "Aargh, I was dropped. I didn't want to feel this way! But it's my story."

Maybe you moved around all the time. Your parents would uproot you, and you had a hard time maintaining friendships or developing a real connection. This follows you into adulthood. Or, maybe for you, as a young child, he left. Or, she left. You grew up without Dad. Or, you grew up without Mom. You didn't choose that. You didn't ask for it. But, in that part of your life, you were dropped. A part of you became crippled and broken, and it has defined your story to this day.

Possibly there was abuse or neglect. Maybe you were hurt, robbed, stolen from...whatever it is...everyone has a story. When

CHAPTER 6: DO UNTO OTHERS

I meet you, I want you to judge me in light of my story. I want you to be aware of my background—that I grew up in a small town in the middle of Wyoming with a relatively low income family and three other siblings all about the same age—and how that created so much of my story. I want you to know all of those parts of my story, so that when you see me doing the things that I do or reacting the way that I react, you might give me the benefit of the doubt, because I have a story. We all want that. We want people to understand us and treat us in response to the story that we have. We all want that, but if we're honest, it's a lot harder to give someone that benefit. We don't take time to learn their story; the story of how they became crippled.

There's a principle in life called the law of negative attribution or the fundamental attribution error, as Lee Ross coined the phrase.[55] This principle means that if you see someone in the grocery store yelling at their kids, you blame it on their character. You just say, "Well, that's a bad mom. I mean, who would ever treat their kids like that." But, if you have a similar situation where you're yelling at your kids in the store, you will attribute it, not to your character, but to your environment. You will say, "I've had such a long day, and I'm working too many hours. My husband is constantly gone and not helping me at all." All these reasons led you to do what you did and you attribute your action (or reaction) to the story. With someone else, we attribute it to their character.

Do you see why it's such an important principle of grace to remember that everyone has a story? Everyone's been dropped. Everyone has a place in their life where they could say, "I'm

---

55. Berkowitz, L. (1977). *Advances in Experimental Social Psychology*, 10. New York, NY: Academic Press.

crippled in both feet, and it's become a part of my identity." This isn't an excuse for our behavior, but if we can understand the story and how it has shaped our identity, we begin to see why we do what we do. This is Mephibosheth's story.

Look at 2 Samuel 9:5 and see what happens next.

> *So David sent for him and brought him from Makir's home. His name was Mephibosheth; he was Jonathan's son and Saul's grandson. When he came to David he bowed low to the ground in deep respect. David said, "Greetings Mephibosheth." Mephibosheth replied, "I am your servant."*
>
> *"Don't be afraid," David said.*[56]

Now think for a moment about this scenario. Why did David have to say, "Don't be afraid?" Because Mephibosheth had every reason to be afraid! At this point, Mephibosheth had been living for the past 15-20 years in a place called Lo Debar; pasture-less, out of bounds—a place where no one can see him. He has lived all those years hoping that no one remembers his name and that no one in Jerusalem knows he's alive. He hopes that he's been forgotten, so that he can live out his days in peace.

But one day, there's a knock at the door, and the gruff shouting of a royal soldier: "King David wants to see you." What emotions, do you think, filled his heart and mind in this moment? "I've been found. He knows I'm alive. I'm as good as dead!" Mephibosheth is brought to the palace, to the place he never wanted to see again. But there he is, brought before David, the reigning king of all the land. Mephibosheth is filled with fear—for good reason—because

---

56. 2 Samuel 9:5-7

CHAPTER 6: DO UNTO OTHERS

he knows what everyone else knows: he should be killed so that David can preserve his line and secure his claim to the throne. How could he not be afraid of the king who held such rightful authority over him?

Which leads to our second principle of grace: **Everyone grapples with fear.**

Everyone grapples with fear because somewhere in our life there is a place where we could be rightfully condemned. We might try and object, but if we look inside we know it to be true. If our secrets were known—if it was completely known to you the things I have done and why—you could look at me and say, "That was wrong and I condemn you." And I would have to say, "You're right. I'm worthy of being condemned."

If we could see that others have this right with us and our behaviors, how much more so with God Almighty? The thought that I could stand before God and have Him judge the thoughts and attitudes in every motive of my heart is a frightening proposition. In that place, I would have no defense but to say to Him, "You're right." For that reason, everyone of us, in some way, grapples with the fear of exposure; the fear of being judged or condemned. If my hidden behaviors were known—if the attitudes or thoughts of my mind were made clear—I could be judged and condemned, and rightfully so.

We fear this happening. This is an important principle of grace. If we understand that this is universal, then suddenly it removes us from being the standard of grace. We know there are places in our life that if we were brought before the king and all was made known, he could say, "To your death." And everyone else would say, "Well that's what they deserved."

If everyone grapples with fear and everyone has a story, it puts us in the same place as Mephibosheth.

> *"Don't be afraid!" David says. I intend to show kindness to you because of my promise to your father, Jonathan. I will give you all the property that once belonged to your grandfather Saul, and you will eat here with me at the king's table!"*
>
> *Mephibosheth bowed respectfully and exclaimed, "Who is your servant that you should show such kindness to a dead dog like me?"*[57]

Did you hear that? Mephibosheth knows he's a dead dog. He should be killed. David should do it. But David looks at him and says, "Mephibosheth, I'm going to show kindness to you, but not because of you. I'm going to show kindness to you because of your father."

That, my friends, is the third principle of grace: **The basis of grace is not the person in front of us, but the Father above us.**

David shows extraordinary kindness to Mephibosheth in this story, not because Mephibosheth deserved or warranted grace. Mephibosheth hadn't been good enough, or kind enough to others for David to say, "Okay, I'll show you kindness." David says, "I'm showing you kindness for one reason. It's because of your father, Jonathan, and what he did for me."

A quick summary reveals a great story in the friendship between Jonathan and David. At a young age they became the

---

57. 2 Samuel 9:7-8

CHAPTER 6: DO UNTO OTHERS

closest of friends and buddies. In this story, on a couple of different occasions, it is Jonathan who saves David's life from Jonathan's own father, Saul. In fact, at one point, Jonathan comes to David when he's in hiding and says, "I will protect you. One day, David, you will be king, and I will stand beside you and serve you."[58] This is a beautiful picture to us even now, here in our day and age. But for Jonathan to say it at that time in history was pure foolishness. He should have been saying, "Listen David, I'm the next king. You better show me respect. You better serve me." But Jonathan loved David so much, and he could see that God had picked David, so he was okay with it. He said, "David, when you're king, I will serve you gladly and gratefully. Only, let's make this covenant, that we will take care of one another's ancestors."[59] And David responded, "For your sake, I will." Based on that story—and that story alone—David finds Mephibosheth and says, "I'm going to pour out kindness and grace on you. Not because of you, but because of your father and what he's done for me."

Does that sound like something we would say to others? Our spouse may not deserve grace from us. Our kids may not deserve grace from us. Our mother-in-law may not deserve grace from us. But grace is not about them. The basis for grace is not the person in front of you but the Father who stands above you. We can look to Him and say, "God, show me how much you have done for me, so that I can go and show that grace to one of Your children."

Look what happens back in the text. So, Mephibosheth says, *"Why would you do this to a dead dog,"* and it's almost like David doesn't hear him! King David summons Ziba (2 Samuel

---

58. 1 Samuel 23:15-18
59. 1 Samuel 20:14-17

9:9). Remember Ziba? Of course, because we've heard his name about 18 times already! Ziba, Ziba, Ziba. And David says to him, *"I have given your master's grandson everything that belonged to Saul and his family."* Now we don't know exactly how much it is, but I'm guessing the king's family had a lot; a lot of land, a lot of buildings, a lot of gold. David, in one fell swoop, says, "I'm giving it ALL to Mephibosheth." And what's more, Ziba, *"You and your sons and servants are to farm the land for him and to produce food for your master's household. But Mephibosheth, your master's grandson, will eat here at my table."*[60]

Then, in parenthesis, we get this great note: Ziba had 15 sons and 20 servants. Overnight, Mephibosheth went from being a poor crippled guy living in the middle of nowhere to waking up in the palace with 35 servants at his command, with land and money to spare. Although he had nothing, he now has everything.

This is the fourth principle of grace: **Grace is always extravagant.**

Grace is always too much. David gave a crippled man a king's reward. All the land, all the money, all the servants, and a place at the king's table to boot. It would have been enough—in fact, it would have been more than enough—if David would have found Mephibosheth, called him to his palace and said, "Listen, Mephibosheth, you know that I could rightfully kill you because you are of the former monarchy. But because of your father, Jonathan, I'm going to spare you. Go and live in peace." And Mephibosheth would have said, "Thank you. To know that I don't have to hide or run anymore…" That would have been more than enough. But, David doesn't stop there. David says, "Not only am I

---

60. 2 Samuel 9:10

CHAPTER 6: DO UNTO OTHERS

going to spare your life, I want to give you all the land and all the riches and all the servants Saul had, and you can eat at my table and live in my palace. You can have it all."

When you think about the grace God gives you and me, it would have been enough for Him to do far less than He did. Through faith, when we came to Christ, God could have come to us and said, "Because of your faith, when it comes to the end of your life, you know what? I'll take it easy on you. I'll only judge you for some of the wrong things you've done. I'll only make you pay a little bit. I'll go really light on you." That would have been enough. It would have been enough if God would have said, "Because of Christ, I'll forgive your sin and spare your life, but that's about it."

I'd take that deal! But God didn't stop there. He said, "I'm going to forgive your sin. In fact, I'll forgive them all; past, present, and future. I'm going to put a huge stamp of grace on your soul, 'forgiven.' But that's not all! Next, I'm going to wrap you in the righteousness of Christ so that when I see you, I don't actually see your righteousness, I see the righteousness of My son, Jesus, and so I'll pronounce over you 'righteous.' Then, I'm going to pour my Holy Spirit into your life; I'm literally going to come and live in you. Your body's going to be My temple, and everywhere you go, I will be with you. I'm going to give you peace that surpasses understanding, and I'm going to give you joy that the world doesn't understand. I'm going to call you My child. Then, I'm going to give you eternity; and in eternity, you're going to sit at My right hand with Jesus and reign with Him. There will be endless celebration. No more tears or sorrows or fears; no more sickness or death. I'm giving you all of it." Doesn't something inside you say, "HOLY COW!"

It would have been enough if the Lord would have just said, "I'll let you off easy." But He gave us all so much. Grace is always extravagant. Here, we're given a picture of God's incredible grace to us.

Now look at how the story ends. In verse 11, Ziba replies to David's command. I picture this with a bit of sarcasm, because up to this point, Ziba and his sons were farming the land for their own good. Now they have a master they have to serve. Later in 2 Samuel, we find Ziba acting a little underhanded, trying to get the land back for himself. So, sarcasm included, Ziba replied, *"Yes, my lord the king; I am your servant, and I will do all that you have commanded." And from that time on, Mephibosheth ate regularly at David's table, like one of the king's own sons. Mephibosheth had a young son named Mica. From then on, all the members of Ziba's household were Mephibosheth's servants. And Mephibosheth, who was crippled in both feet,* (Notice that didn't change. He still has his infirmity.) *lived in Jerusalem and ate regularly at the king's table."*[61]

How many times in those last four verses do we find that Mephibosheth will be eating at David's table? In every verse, over and over; "eating at my table, will eat at my table, is eating at my table..." We get the picture. Remember what we learned earlier: Scripture is not written like a newspaper story. It's not just an article, reporting what happened. It's written with intent. When you see something repeated like this four times, something in our head should go off, "Ding! This is important." But why is it so important?

To be brought to David's table was the ultimate kindness. This invitation boldly declares, "Not only am I going to give you

---

61. 2 Samuel 9:11-13

CHAPTER 6: DO UNTO OTHERS

all these things, I'm going to treat you like you're one of my own. I'm going to give you a place with my own sons. When I look to my right, I will see my blood sons, and when I look to my left, I will see you, my adopted son, eating at the same place."

And this is the fifth principle of grace: **Grace creates relationship.**

Grace is always an invitation to relationship; to a place of belonging that says, "Not only will I be kind, not only will I be extravagant in what I give to you, but I will invite you to have a place at the table where you are treated like family." That's what David has given to Mephibosheth, and that's what our God has given to us through Christ. God not only pours out His loving kindness on us, He's brought us to His table and says, "Eat with Me. Belong to Me. You are one of My very own. I want you here."

Remember at the end of the last chapter how I said that confession is only a beginning, the opening of a door? This is why. The goal of confession—of being fully known in all our stuff—is that we might move into relationship. Mephibosheth stood before David with nothing to hide. And in that place of ultimate vulnerability, the king lavishes love and goodness on him. His ultimate vulnerability led to a place of ultimate love and acceptance. Confession is the beginning. Whole-hearted relationship with God and others is the end goal.

The great thing about this story is that every single one of us is invited to find ourselves in Mephibosheth's story. We can know that the God of Heaven sees our story, and He doesn't judge us for the story. He sees that we could be rightfully condemned, but instead, through Christ, He gives us grace. It's extravagant, and it creates ongoing relationship with Him: Father, Son and Holy Spirit.

But, that's not the end of the story. You see, we're not meant to see ourselves only as Mephibosheth.

We are also meant to see ourselves as a *type* of David.

There's this beautiful thread throughout Scripture. The King David of this story becomes the family line of Jesus Christ. And all who are in Jesus Christ, become family as well, of David and Jesus, all the way down to us. There is a place in your world where you have the possibility to be David to others. Taking all that God has poured on us, in His extravagant grace and love, and say, "Lord, not because of what they've done and not because of what they deserve, but because of You and what You've given to me, I will give extravagant grace to them."

That is what a culture of grace is all about. A culture of grace is created when I give to others what I have been given by God. I give, not because they deserve it or have earned it or proved they are worthy, but simply because I look to God and say, "Lord, look what You've given to me. Help me give it to them." A culture of grace takes what we've been given and gives it to others. We become a conduit of God's grace.

I want to give you an illustration of how I think this can happen and how I think we can grow in this. I owe this illustration to Sundar Krishnan, the brother-in-law of Ravi Zacharias, and a pastor, writer and speaker. It has also been published in the book, *The Gospel-Centered Life*.[62]

When we come to faith in Christ, there is a development in our lives that is intended to happen. As we see God, and approach Him in His Word and in prayer, we grow in our appreciation of His holiness. We cultivate more and more of a "wow" factor; saying, "Lord, look what You've done. Look who You are: Your

---

62. Thune, R. & Walker, W. (2011). *The Gospel-Centered Life: Leader's Guide*. Greensboro, NC: New Growth Press.

CHAPTER 6: DO UNTO OTHERS

majesty, Your might, Your strength, Your power, Your glory, Your eternal nature." This awareness is constantly growing.

What happens at the same time is a growing awareness of our own sinfulness. I become more deeply aware of my brokenness and my pride. The deepest inclinations of my heart can so easily stray away from God and on to myself. The gap created between these two dynamics—His holiness and my sinfulness—can be very painful. But what happens, when this takes place, is that the cross of Jesus Christ gets bigger and bigger. His cross covers that gap between what we see in God and what we see in ourselves. We look to the cross, the good news, and we are able to say, "Thank you, Jesus, for saving a wretch like me. I once was lost, and when I found You, I didn't even know how lost I was. But the more I get to know You and Your holiness, the more in awe I am of Your cross because I'm aware of my sinfulness."

This is why the apostle Paul—a pastor and church planter for over 25 years—in his letter to a young pastor named Timothy says, "I am the worst of sinners."[63] Worst of sinners? Paul, you're writing the Bible! How bad can you be? Is it that he was getting worse and worse? No. It's that this picture was taking place in his life: The more he encountered God and His holiness, the more aware he was of the evil and depravity of his own heart, apart from God, and the more in love he was with the cross.

But something else can happen. We can come to faith in Christ, but instead of being more and more aware of God's holiness, we feel the need to perform. My eyes aren't really on God. My eyes are on how well am I doing; whether or not I am following the rules and doing what I am supposed to do. It's really not about God anymore. It's about how well I am doing. As soon as we get into that, we're not more aware of our sinfulness, we are more prone to hide it and to live in pretense. We pretend that we are better than we are and hide the stuff that's bad, acting like we've got it all together when we don't.

In this category, the danger is that the cross doesn't get bigger and bigger. The cross actually gets smaller and smaller. In this place, there's no room for the cross. There is only room for what I can do and how I can do it better. If we want to know whether or not we are going to be people of grace, it leads us to one question: *Is the cross getting bigger or smaller in your life?*

Are you becoming more and more aware of what you've been forgiven and how much God's grace and mercy means to you? Or is the cross more and more in the rear view mirror, getting smaller and smaller? If we get stuck in the performance track, we might even talk ourselves into thinking, "I deserve to be saved. God really needs me. I'm doing pretty well."

---

63. 1 Timothy 1:15 NKJV

CHAPTER 6: DO UNTO OTHERS

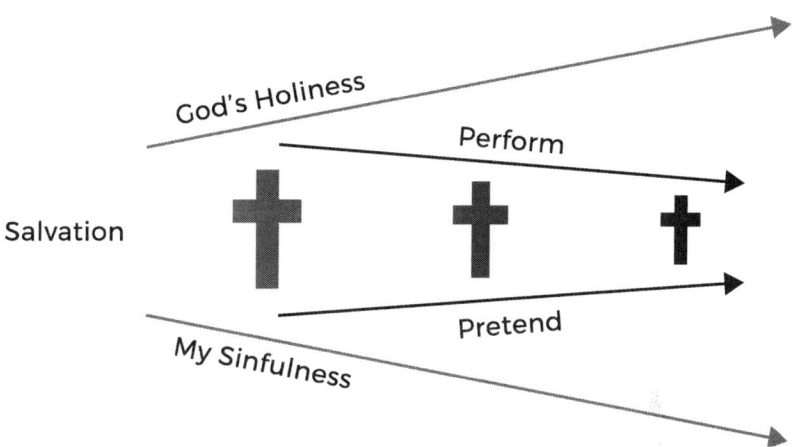

When we're stuck in this mindset, it's almost impossible for us to give grace to anyone else. We are wound up so tightly, trying to prove that we deserve grace, that we certainly can't give others the grace of God. But if we live in the first picture, and the cross is getting bigger and bigger, then when we meet someone else, we just say, "Here...here, look what He gave me. I didn't deserve it anymore than you ever will. In fact, I'm the chief of sinners. Here...let me give you what He gave me."

My friends, a culture of grace is created when we give to others what we've been given by God. Is His cross growing bigger or is it getting smaller? If we want to live in a way where the cross is getting bigger and bigger for us, then take these four steps today:

1. FIX YOUR EYES ON THE FATHER.

When we start our day thinking about Him, it's amazing how much easier it is for us to have grace for others. But if my eyes are only on you, it's really hard for me to be gracious because I so easily see your problems. If I'm thinking about God, His holiness and what He's done for me, I can respond to you from that grace-filled state of mind. Then, if you come to me and say, "Nick, I made this mistake. Listen to what happened." It's so much easier for me to respond, "That's okay. Look what God gave me. Let me give it to you."

But if my thoughts are on you, and I'm thinking about how you've hurt me or how I hope you'll do better, grace won't be my natural response. If you come to me and confess something, then my attitude says, "I don't want to be gracious. You deserve what you're going to get." If we want to be grace-givers, we must first fix our eyes on the Father.

Pastor and author Andy Stanley has said, "The more aware I am of the work God still has to do in me, the less critical I am of the work God still has to do in you."[64] As we stay in a place of being known by God, we allow Him to do a deep work in our life *first*. And when I experience grace for my stuff, I can give you grace for yours.

2. REMEMBER THE DEPTH OF HIS FORGIVENESS.

By this, I don't mean that we go out and wallow in our sin: "I'm the worst person. I'm terrible. If I just remember how terrible I am, then I can give grace." I don't mean that. Wallowing is actually a twisted version of performance—we have to be bad enough to really deserve grace!

What I am referring to is the healthy awe and wonder over the fact that God would even choose to forgive me. The woman in Luke 7 encountered this kind of grace. Jesus had been invited to lunch at the home of a Pharisee named Simon. A woman

---

64. Andy Stanley Leadership Podcast. Retrieved from https://itunes.apple.com/us/podcast/andy-stanley-leadership-podcast/id290055666?mt=2

CHAPTER 6: DO UNTO OTHERS

comes in—a prostitute—and anoints Jesus with perfume. Simon is very judgmental, thinking that if Jesus, a prophet, knew who she was, then he wouldn't let her touch him. But Jesus answered Simon's thoughts:

"Simon," *he said to the Pharisee, "I have something to say to you." "Go ahead, Teacher," Simon replied. Then Jesus told him this story: "A man loaned money to two people—500 pieces of silver to one and 50 pieces to the other. But neither of them could repay him, so he kindly forgave them both, canceling their debts. Who do you suppose loved him more after that?" Simon answered, "Well, I suppose the one for whom he canceled the larger debt." "That's right," Jesus said. Then he turned to the woman* (picture Jesus looking at her as he's talking to Simon) *and said to Simon, "Look at this woman kneeling here. When I entered your home, you didn't offer me water to wash the dust from my feet, but she has washed them with her tears and wiped them with her hair. You didn't greet me with a kiss, but from the time I first came in, she has not stopped kissing my feet. You neglected me the courtesy of olive oil to anoint my head, but she has anointed my feet with rare perfume. I tell you, her sins—and they are many—* (Jesus was not ignoring the sin) *have been forgiven, so she has shown me much love. But a person who is forgiven little, shows only little love." Then Jesus said to the woman, "Your sins are forgiven." The men at the table said among themselves, "Who is this man, that he goes around forgiving sins." And Jesus said to the woman, "Your faith has saved you; go in peace."*[65]

Now on the day this occurred, as the Pharisees went back to their homes, and the woman that anointed Jesus with perfume

---

65. Luke 7:40-50

went back to her home, which one do you think was more gracious after that? It's obvious, right? The woman who knew she'd been forgiven, knew she had a lot to be forgiven of, would be the one to offer forgiveness to others.

Friends, that's where grace comes from in our lives. We are gracious, not because we conjure it up or try really hard to be gracious, but because we stay in touch with what Jesus showed us in His forgiveness. The more we live in that bigger cross, the more gracious our response.

At some point, if we're doing it right, we ought to feel like we're being too gracious. There's something about our full giving of grace that allows truth to be know as well. All too often, we are afraid that if we give too much grace, then others won't have to face the truth. But the amazing paradox of Scripture is that when God's grace is fully given, people's eyes are opened to the truth and they are actually able to change.

3. ACTIVELY SEEK OPPORTUNITIES TO PASS ON HIS GRACE.

David's proactivity is what's great about this story: David doesn't wait to hear about Mephibosheth. Someone doesn't have to come and say, "Hey, we hear there's a relative of Saul that's alive. Weren't you friends with his dad, Jonathan?" Mephibosheth doesn't have to come to David. David is the one seeking out Mephibosheth and asking the question, "Is there anyone to whom I can show kindness?"

What would happen in the church and in our lives if we started to ask God that question? Is there anyone to whom I could show kindness, because I've experienced Your kindness? What if we can say to God, "I know what it's like to grow up in a broken

CHAPTER 6: DO UNTO OTHERS

home. I have experienced Your kindness and Your love. Who can I give it to—who is growing up in a broken home right now?"

"Lord, I know what it is like to experience Your grace coming out of a broken relationship or a divorce, and I'm just so grateful for who You have been in my life. Who could I show kindness to because of the kindness You've given me?"

"Jesus, you have set me free from my addiction. Who do I know that's caught up in their addiction that I could love and support with the strength You gave me?"

Could you ask this question of God: God, who could I show kindness to? He will be faithful to bring someone to mind. When He does, go and actively seek them out.

4. INVITE OTHERS TO THE FATHER'S TABLE.

The ultimate grace is not giving people *your* kindness. The goal is not to leave them saying, "Wow, that Nick; he is such a gracious wonderful guy." That would be a good step. It would be better than having them think what a rotten guy you are!

No, the ultimate kindness would be to have them say, "Look at what God has done for me." In these situations, this means being willing to clearly give credit where credit is due. We say to someone, "I'm giving you all this because of what God has given to me. Because of His grace and love in my life, I can't help but give it to you. Would you like to hear more about it?" As we invite others to the Father's table, and they discover that they belong, they will recognize they have a seat at the Heavenly Father's table. This will transform their lives; not by our grace (because, remember, we are not the basis for grace), but by His. So, invite others to His table.

Thanks to my lawn mowing incident, I've been thinking about "getting what we deserve." When it comes to our Heavenly Father, what do we deserve? Nothing. But what has He given us? Everything. So the person in front of you, what do they deserve? Nothing. But what does your Heavenly Father invite you to give them? Everything. Not because they deserve it, but because you didn't deserve it either and He gave it freely to you. Safe places are created by people who simply walk around saying, "Let me give you what He gave me."

Can you imagine what would happen in our world if every Christ-follower began to operate based on this definition of grace? Can you picture how different the reputation of the church would be? Can you see how the masses of people would run toward the church, hungering for this true grace of God? The lavish grace of God given through the people of God ushers in the Kingdom of God.

May it be so of us.

CHAPTER 7
THE GRACE OF CALLING

In this life, we all answer some very important questions.

- *What do you want to be when you grow up?*
- *Where are you going to college?*
- *Will you marry me?*
- *How many kids do we want to have?*
- *Do you want fries with that?*

Okay, maybe not the last one, but you get the idea. The way we answer these questions become trajectories for our life.

I was 10 years into marriage and ministry, and everything on the outside looked like the ideal of what a young pastor should be. I had a beautiful wife, young children that were thriving, and a church that was growing every year; but I knew something on the inside that few others knew. I was dying inside. The presenting issue was my struggle with pornography. But there were deeper issues that were driving the behavior. During this time in my life I was unaware of them. These issues centered around a pivotal question that I invite you to wrestle with.

I believe this is the most important question you can ever ask as a leader, a parent, a teacher, or a coach. It's the kind of question that at a first glance might seem obvious or even insignificant. But as we dig into it, we will see that the way we answer this question will lead us on one of two very different trajectories with two very different outcomes.

The question is this: *Am I in leadership because I am the most qualified person in the room, or because I am called?*

Am I in leadership, am I doing what I do; am I a pastor, a counselor, a husband or a wife because I'm the most qualified person to do it, or because I have been called by God to do it?

This question has particular importance if we are in a time of preparation—going to school, being trained for a job, or working on some new skill. Seasons of preparation can deceive us into a way of thinking. This way of thinking, if we could confront it directly, would appear obvious and we would know that it is not a biblical perspective. So often it's left in the background of our mind and it subtly drives our thinking and our behavior.

In this question, we are addressing the inner workings of our soul and resetting it so it will run efficiently and properly for many, many years to come. It's like the true north on a compass. When you pull one out to navigate, you assume that north is, well, north. You assume true north can be trusted. But if something has changed true north, like a magnetic pole, and it creates a distortion, we will continually assume we know true north and will be misguided. We are not properly calibrated.

So this question really is a way of recalibrating, setting a true north, for who we are as men and women, as leaders, and as the local church.

CHAPTER 7: THE GRACE OF CALLING

In 1 Chronicles 29, the story is told of King David dedicating the temple and leaving it to his son Solomon to build. Over that temple he prays these words: *Yours, O LORD, is the greatness, the power, the glory, the victory, and the majesty. Everything in the heavens and on earth is yours, O LORD, and this is your kingdom. We adore you as the one who is over all things. Wealth and honor come from you alone, for you rule over everything. Power and might are in your hand, and at your discretion people are made great and given strength.*[66]

Look at that last sentence again: It is at YOUR discretion that people are made great and given strength. If we look through Scripture, we see that all the great leaders led because of God's discretion. They were called. We could look at the call stories of Abraham, Moses, Gideon, David, Elijah, Paul, the 12 Apostles, the list could go on. Every one of them called to a role, not because they were so qualified to do it, but because God looked at them and said, "I am calling you to these things."

Ephesians 2:10 says, *"He has created us...[to] do the good works he planned for us from long ago."* Have you ever thought about that? Before you were even born, before your name popped-up on the screen at the hospital, God had already planned, long ago, the good works that you were going to do.

In 1 Corinthians 1:26-27, God talks about how He chose the foolish things of this world, the things that are not, the things of little regard, to shame the things that are; the wise and the wisdom of this world.

In Ephesians 4:1, the apostle Paul wrote and said, *"Lead a life worthy of your calling."* If you think about that simple phrase, he says the way we live springs from the calling we have

---

66. I Chronicles 29:11-12

received. Notice that it's the performance, the life of excellence we attempt to live, that springs from our calling. Our performance as ministers, counselors, as fathers and mothers, husbands and wives, must spring from our calling, and not be the basis for it.

You see, that's the danger we're in. We were given a job because we received training and got our degree. We get a title and begin to feel like the reason we were given this job, this role, or this title is because we have the degree. We look the part. "I'm so qualified and spiritual! And because I'm spiritual and qualified, they want me to do the things I'm doing." But what it creates in us is fear; a deep-seated fear that they might find out I'm not as spiritual or as qualified or capable as someone else in the room. And if someone else is more qualified than me, why wouldn't they just give them the job?

This is a pattern that I stayed in for many years. I went into ministry right from college at the age of 23. I was an associate pastor for only two and a half years, when the senior pastor decided that he had been called to an international church overseas. Through a season of interim, as I developed some leadership skills, I thought I was just keeping the seat warm for the next senior pastor. Then the elder board came to me and said, "Nick, we think you are our next senior pastor." So at the age of 26, I became "senior" pastor. Something inside of me shifted and said, "I need to BE the senior pastor! I need to look the part and play the part. I need to be the most spiritual person in the room. If I'm not, why am I the senior pastor?"

I began to sing the song, do the dance, and play the part that I thought everybody wanted me to play. Because of this I didn't have permission—I didn't give myself permission—to be real about the things that were eating away at my soul.

CHAPTER 7: THE GRACE OF CALLING

As we look at this question, *"Am I qualified, or am I called?"* we discover three realities that each of us must address.

1. A CHOICE BETWEEN PERFORMANCE OR PROCESS

We must choose either to be a person hung up on performance or to be a person IN process. If we're caught up in performance, we believe we need to hide our mistakes and our flaws. If we allow ourselves to be in process, we get the permission to admit them.

If we're caught up in performance, we must ignore or deny our weaknesses; putting up a shield of defense that shows we know what we're doing, we can handle it. Wherever there is a weakness, we deflect or ignore it because it might expose that we're not qualified. If we're in process, we can understand our weaknesses. We can evaluate them and talk them through with friends and mentors, and be aware of how they will impact our role and leadership.

If I'm hung up on performance, I have an inflated self-assessment. There is a feeling for many in ministry that they are taking a continual selfie and posting it on Facebook so everybody knows, "Look, I'm good enough for this job." If I'm in process, though, I'm allowed to have a humble self-assessment. I can know what I don't know and ask for help and input.

As we looked at in chapter 1, the harsh reality for many ministries and churches is that we want people who have already been *processed*. Think about that. We want people who have already been discipled. They've been through the chaotic journey of change, and now they're ready to serve, give and lead. We want this because to be in process is too messy! To be in process is unpredictable and challenging, so we want people to already be processed. Yet, what this creates is an environment where everyone is compelled to perform and pretend, because the truth is, we're all in process somewhere and somehow.

As you look at the realities of performance versus process, where do you tend to land? What do you feel is expected of you?

2. SUCCESS VERSUS SIGNIFICANCE

Am I pursuing success or significance? If I'm pursuing success, I will always prioritize the things that make me look successful. I'll prioritize the more public things, the things that get the accolade and the praise, the applause and the attaboys. Whereas, if I'm prioritizing significance, I put first the things God has asked me to do, whether or not they are glamorous or ever known by others.

If I'm caught up in success, I will prioritize what leads to personal advancements and growing my kingdom. When I am pursuing significance, I prioritize what leads to advancing His kingdom and furthering God's agenda.

If I'm caught up in success, I hope to be served. I hope to have others do for me the less desirable roles or the things I don't feel like doing. If I'm pursuing significance, I hope to serve. I hope to follow in the pathway of Christ and serve others, even as He came and served us.

Do you see how very different those two pathways are? How very different the trajectory they would take us on as leaders?

3. APPEARANCE VERSUS AUTHENTICITY

Do I value appearance or do a I value authenticity? Appearance always asks the question, "How do I look?" Authenticity asks the question, "Why am I really here? What am I about?" Appearance asks, "How am I coming across? How am I presenting myself?"

CHAPTER 7: THE GRACE OF CALLING

Authenticity asks, "What's His message? What does God want to say to me and through me?"

Appearance gets us caught up in image management, always needing to lift up ourselves. Authenticity is about glorifying God and lifting up others.

My personal belief is that most churches today want to appear authentic. We don't really want to be authentic. Not really. It can be far too messy. But there's something about authenticity that is attractive. We want that feeling of, "Oh, they're so real," but only to a point where everything is still safe and contained. But authenticity is messy.

As a young pastor, one thing I began to realize was that even in authenticity I could look really good. People would ask, "Pastor Nick, how's your week been?" I could be "authentic" and say, "It's been a pretty hard week. I've had to counsel a few marriages in crisis. I've had work to do on this new sermon series. I've had to perform at a funeral (interesting choice of word that we use, isn't it: *performing* weddings and funerals). And I had to travel to present at a conference." Notice how in my attempt to be authentic, "Oh it's been a hard week," I just listed four things that most people in my congregation will never, ever do. They're not going to counsel couples in crisis, write a sermon series, preside at funerals, or travel and present at a conference. So as I give this *authentic* view of how hard my week has been, what it actually creates for them is this feeling; "Wow, listen to all those things our pastor does!" I appear to look good by the very things I use to sound authentic.

Why not just say, "I've had a hard week because I have stretched myself too thin." With this kind of admissions they could relate, "Oh, I've had that kind of week, too!"

As we look at this question, "Why am I in leadership—because I'm qualified or called?" this is the truth: You cannot serve two masters. Jesus talked about this in terms of God and money, but the same is true here. We can't simultaneously be the most qualified, spiritual person in the room and also remain focused on our calling.

The two will not live together. Nor should they.

The bottom line is this: When we are not authentic, it's because of fear and shame. As previously discussed, shame says there is something wrong with me. Guilt, on the other hand, says I did something wrong. I made a mistake or did something I regret and wish I hadn't. But shame interprets guilt to say that the reason I did what I didn't want to do, the reason I made that mistake, is because there's something wrong with me. I not only do wrong; I am wrong.

To use a football analogy, guilt is like getting a 15-yard penalty for unnecessary roughness; shame is a belief that I don't even belong on the team. Shame will always create a fear of being found out or exposed for who I really am. I fear that you will reject me if you discover the real me. My shame tells me there's something wrong with me, that I have choices, traits, or flaws that I need to hide or ignore. This internal belief leads me to project an image, but even with the image intact, I remain fearful that you'll see through my facade to the real me. So I must repair all the cracks and keep the image looking good to avoid being discovered.

A book came out in the 90's with the title: *Why Am I Afraid to Tell You Who I Am?* The author's answer in the book is, "Because I'm afraid if you knew me, you'd reject me. And this is all I've got!"[67]

---

[67]. Powell, J. (1995). *Why Am I Afraid to Tell You Who I Am?: Insights into Personal Growth.* Chicago, IL: Thomas More Association.

CHAPTER 7: THE GRACE OF CALLING

Think about that for a moment: I'm afraid that if you knew me you would reject me and this is all I've got! So I posture and pose, I pretend. Why? So that you'll like me. Only, when you do like me, I don't receive it because I am led to believe the only reason you like me is because of what I postured, posed and pretended! The real me remains unknown and unaddressed. So even when you love me, or say you like me and approve of me, something inside whispers, "It's only because they don't know the real you." The fear of being discovered, and rejected, keeps me stuck in that performance-driven, success-driven, appearance-driven way of leading.

Remember the illustration from chapter 2 on the Public Me vs. the Private Me?

When the truth of Jesus and His grace becomes real, not just to our head—to know the right thing—but into our heart, where we begin to believe the truth about who we are, this makes all the difference.

We can come back to the divide between the Public and Private Me, but remember, all that truly matters is Christ in me; His call. If Christ in me is what matters, then I have the freedom to be real with you and to pursue my call out of the real me.

This is who we are: Christ in us!

The reason we end up in ministry, or counseling, or on staff at a church—the reason we do what we do—is not because we are so qualified to do it, but because Christ in us calls us to do it. He looked at you and He looked at me from long ago and declared, "Here are the good works I created for you to do." With this knowledge, we can walk into any situation as authentic people trusting that God made us to do this!

There's an old leadership adage by Lee Iacocca that, while trite in some regards, rings true in this area: the speed of the leader is the speed of the team.

In other words, for better or worse, who we are as leaders will be reproduced throughout our ministry context or our environment. You teach what you know, but you reproduce who you are. You can teach all the brilliant things you know, and everyone will nod along and say, "Thank you pastor, counselor, or teacher, that was such wonderful information!"

But it's who you are that they will replicate. It's who you are that they will imitate.

I have noticed this in my family with my wife and kids. When I come home grumpy or preoccupied by an unresolved situation at work, if I begin to respond to my wife and kids in anger, guess what I begin to see in them? Anger. Harsh words and critical responses. I suddenly find this mirror reflecting back to me my own negativity. My loved ones, taking their cues from my behavior, are simply behaving like me.

We don't want to heap unfair responsibility on ourselves to try and control everyone else's behavior. Their response is still their responsibility; but we must recognize that we create change, not just by what we do, but by who we are. This is the most consistent way to shape a culture. If you walk into a situation as an authentic

CHAPTER 7: THE GRACE OF CALLING

person, without your carefully crafted image of doing the dance and singing the song, and instead you acknowledge your weaknesses and admit your faults, asking for help, and inviting participation, others begin to do the same. Authenticity is first and foremost a leadership issue.

We must avoid the convenient excuse that this is someone else's responsibility. If they would just change. If that church would get more real. If people would stop faking it. If only she would be honest. If only he would do this differently. No, no, and no! Authenticity begins with me. Authenticity and humility is leadership. To be authentic about your weaknesses is leadership. To be humble about what you can and cannot do—to acknowledge your weaknesses and mistakes IS leadership.

How did Jesus lead? How did Jesus model this?

He lived a sinless life, and so He had no mistakes or weakness to own. Yet, look at the attitude that marked His life. Philippians 2:6-8 (NIV) *"Who (Jesus), being in very nature God, did not consider equality with God something to be used to his own advantage; rather he made himself nothing by taking the very nature of a servant, being made in human likeness. And being found in appearance as a man, he humbled himself by becoming obedient to death—even death on a cross!"*

When we look at all this, we can only conclude what Jesus did in coming to our world—the way He humbled Himself and gave up His life—this was leadership! We have been invited to walk and live the same way.

FOUR PRACTICES TO CREATE A PLACE OF AUTHENTICITY

So, how does this happen? How do we truly create a place of authenticity? This all sounds good until we actually begin to go and do it. When the rubber hits the road, authenticity suddenly feels difficult, chaotic, and even unsafe. In light of this, where do we begin?

1. WE MUST CONTINUALLY FIGHT AGAINST CELEBRITY CULTURE.

Our culture continually pushes us in this direction of celebrity. I am not only referring to the megachurch, where the pastor, turned celebrity, has his own jet and mansion. We can easily sit back and take pot shots at this scenario. The deeper truth, however, is that we have a celebrity culture *inside* of ourselves.

Celebrity culture says, "My position comes from my performance. Therefore I must always perform so I can keep my position." That's what a celebrity is—a projected image that makes us watch the movies and consume the product they want us to buy. So the celebrity must forever keep creating that image or reproduce the performance, otherwise they won't have the role. We would quit buying whatever it is they are selling.

When a "celebrity culture" lives in us, we make decisions about what we wear, what we say, and what we participate in based on how it makes us look. We do, say, or wear something because it makes us look good; and this feels good. So we keep on doing it, whether our interior life matches up or not. The truth is, celebrity culture is an exhausting cycle because we must always be on guard.

CHAPTER 7: THE GRACE OF CALLING

The key here is to move toward awareness; awareness of when this is happening and I feel myself powering up, putting on the mask, doing the dance and singing the song. When I become aware and feel this happening, I must stop and ponder, "Why do I think I need to perform for this person? Why do I think I need to be something I'm not? Why do I think I need to act differently from who I am?" In this awareness, we discern the subtle voice of deception that says, "I'm afraid if I don't perform, they'll reject me. They won't like me." When we pick up on this, we can begin to respond differently; "No, that's not why I'm here—to protect myself! I'm here because my Creator called me. So, God what do you want me to do?" Through awareness, we can drop the act and live without the mask.

2. WE MUST LEAD OUR LEADERS INTO AUTHENTICITY.

Lead our leaders. Sounds like a practice only needed by the heavy hitters or the big guns in ministry. Maybe as you read that, you don't feel like you have other leaders under you. But the truth is, as a human being, at some point in your life you will be leading other leaders. Whether you are leading your children, are in an organization, or are part of a church staff—in some way you will have leadership and others will be looking to you for their cues. And then, they will go out and live in front of others the way they have watched you live.

In that place, you must be willing to lead in authenticity. Sometimes, when we get assigned a role as *leader*, because of our job, our role, or our family situation, we feel a heightened pressure to perform. "Now that I'm leading," we think, "I've really got to show that I know my stuff!" Rather than powering up in order to prove our worth, we actually need to let down our guard and let the cracks show.

Perhaps in your small group, at a board meeting, or around the family dinner table, it could mean taking time to talk; to really talk. Be bold and patient enough to ask, "How is everyone doing? Really? I know we have business to do and things to decide, but first let's talk about what's really happening in our lives."

Or maybe as a decision is being made, going around the table and saying, "Could we just talk about how everyone is feeling about this decision? What's going on inside your head right now? Tell us a little about it."

Then, to set the tone, you go first!

You say, "Let me be honest. Here's what I'm feeling: I'm really worried, or fearful." What you'll find is that as you open that door, others walk through it.

A Note on Bad Boards:

Some of you may be in a situation where you believe this idea of authenticity is a bad, bad idea because of the culture of your board or organization. I don't know your context or your board, but my guess is that you fear talking this way would only lead to rejection, or worse, being fired. Maybe they've made it clear that certain behaviors and weaknesses are not okay. Their words convey that they expect you to perform at a certain level, real or not. That's what I'm referring to as a bad board. A place where authenticity would not be welcome.

Let me give you three quick ideas:

- Start small. There is likely one other person on that board with whom you could begin to be authentic. Meet for coffee or breakfast and ask permission to talk about real stuff, "Could I open up my heart to you?" As you learn to walk in authenticity with this person, the two of you can strategize how to transform the culture of the board on which you serve.

- Invest deeply in a few. Maybe the people you are able to be authentic with are not on the board or the team. You can begin to meet with them—walk together and do life with them—and create a culture of grace. This becomes leadership development.

- Do leadership development from the side. Those in whom you have invested will frequently be the very ones who invest back in your culture and join your board! Maybe the people who are currently in leadership aren't able to be authentic, but as you invest in a few and develop them, they become the board. They join the team and work alongside of you. This is a long-range view of board transition, but can be very effective for those who are committed to staying in their current context.

3. ALLOW AUTHENTICITY TO MAKE IT UP FRONT.

In the church service. In the small group. In the ministry team meeting. Authenticity needs to make it on the stage. I don't mean that leaders should be raw and bleeding all over people. The church worship service is not a therapy session for the pastor.

I am also not suggesting, by any means, that you turn the most recent crisis into this weekend's testimony time; "Oh, last night Joe yelled at his kids. Joe, come up and tell us about that. Let's talk!" That's not appropriate.

So many testimonies, though, sound a lot like this pattern—I was a wreck, Jesus found me, and now things are great. Awesome as this is, it can leave many thinking: "Really, it all just went away? It all got better?" And, if everything didn't get better for us, if the bad habits didn't go away or the relationship is still a mess, we look at our lives and wonder what's wrong with us.

We need to present stories that are still in process. This way, people get to see how God is at work *along the way.*

I watched the power of this from a front-row seat in my life. I was 10 years into my ministry and my marriage when my struggle with pornography brought our marriage to a breaking point. I had allowed the behavior to continue for a decade because I continually convinced myself that it was getting better, and that I had everything under control. I never lived a double-life or hoarded some secret stash. I had this battle where once a month, maybe every other month, I would find myself veering back onto the website or the channels I promised I would never go to again.

I always had this deep sense of honesty and couldn't live with my secret very long. Sooner or later, I would spill to my wife and get it off my chest. I would hear myself saying the same lines like, "I'm so sorry. This isn't about you. It's not because you're not beautiful enough. It's my struggle. I am working on it. It's actually getting better." I would say whatever I could to make her feel better. Yet, I would watch as my wife was hurting more and more, no matter what line I gave. I felt like I was sinning less, but causing greater pain. By 2010, the pain in her life had reached the point where she was ready to leave me. Not because she hated me, but because she hated how I made her feel. She didn't know how to be around the pain I was causing. So in February of that year, I was holding onto my marriage for dear life and with it my kids, my ministry, and everything that was valuable to me.

CHAPTER 7: THE GRACE OF CALLING

It was then that we were introduced to the ministry of Pure Desire. My wife and I walked through a time of intentional counseling with therapists there, and also joined weekly small groups where we were able to be authentic and real. Over the course of 11 months, God did an amazing work in our lives. We learned how to talk to each other. I learned how to be honest about not just what I did, but to face the deeper issues and emotions that were driving my hurtful behaviors. I discovered how all my needs to perform and be good enough—to look the part—had created hidden places where I didn't know how to deal with the pain or the sense of failure.

As we walked through this process, God was delivering and changing us from the inside out. Over a year later, a new authenticity began for us. I was preaching on the topic of cravings, using Romans 7 and echoing the words of Paul, "Why do I do what I don't want to do? On that Sunday morning, I said, "Friends, this morning I have a unique perspective on this issue because of my addiction to pornography." I went on to share with them how I had struggled. I asked their forgiveness and I invited their help in starting groups in our church so that we could help other men and women who were struggling with a sexual or love addiction.

Many had warned me, "When you get this honest Nick, when you start to put that out there, some people will run away. They won't be able to handle this level of reality from their pastor. They want you to be perfect whether they say it or not."

I actually found the opposite to be true. As I laid down my guard and got real, asking for help and forgiveness, people ran toward me. Something about my struggle gave other people the permission to follow suit. For weeks, they lined up after services to say, "I want to be part of that. If you can be real, and you're the pastor, then so can I!"

I have discovered that every person who came to my church was asking the question, "Can I be loved? Do you love me for who I am, really?" So for years, while I was busy playing the part and putting on a show, so were they. I led them to believe this is what it meant to be a church. It really wasn't safe to reveal the things going on in their minds and what was on their hearts. But when the pastor could stand up and say, "This is me. I've been an addict," they could say, "Wow, there's hope for me, too!"

From that point on, God began to do a beautiful work in our church, simply because people found out it was okay to not be okay. We have to allow that type of authenticity to make it up front.

A Word on Authentic Versus Excellent:

Sometimes in our church or ministry, we think that these two words are on opposite ends of a spectrum. We can either do something really excellent, and that starts to feel showy, or we can do something authentic, off-the-cuff and real. My experience and observation would say that this is not a true spectrum. Authentic and excellent are not opposites.

The weekend I shared honestly and openly with my church was the most programmed, scripted and carefully crafted service we had ever done. We thought about the songs more than we ever had. I wrote out my sermon word for word (which I never did), so I would say it accurately. We crafted who would come up next, who would share, and what invitation would be given at the end. It was programmed to be excellent in every way AND it was authentic: more authentic than we had ever been on a Sunday morning! You can demonstrate authenticity with excellence and plan it well, thinking through the impact of the honesty. It's not one or the other.

CHAPTER 7: THE GRACE OF CALLING

4. WE MUST PASSIONATELY PURSUE GRACE AND TRUTH.

The fourth and final practice of an authentic culture is a 100 percent commitment to both grace and truth. Scripture says that Jesus came full of grace and truth.[68] It wasn't 50/50. It's not that He was half gracious and half truthful. He didn't pick when to be truthful and when to be gracious. "Hmm...this time I'll go with grace, 'You're forgiven!' This time I'll pick truth, 'Depart from me I never knew you!'" In His life, He was all grace AND all truth.

We need to invite that into our churches, small groups, and family. In this environment, we can declare that people are loved and accepted for who they are and also speak the truth about their behavior. Because love, grace, and acceptance are being spoken on a regular basis, you have the freedom to face the truth and do the hard work that needs to be done.

How can you invite all grace and all truth in your church culture? To me, it comes back to this question; not just for the leader but for every person in the church or ministry.

Why am I here? Am I here because I am qualified to be, or am I here because I am called?

Let me tell you, leading out of your calling is extremely liberating. I don't worry about if I am more spiritual than all of my elders, or fear that they find out I don't know what I'm talking about. Instead, I know that I am the pastor because God called me to be. Then I can welcome that there are people in the room that are more spiritual than I am. I can actually celebrate their strengths and utilize them for the good of the body; rather than

---

68. John 1:14

feeling like I must compete with them to show that I am the top and that's why I get paid to be the pastor. When you let go of your need to be the most spiritual, it is then that you begin to do real ministry with real people. And that, my friends, is where it's at!

Are you in leadership because you are the most qualified person in the room? So they picked you!

Or are you in leadership because you are called BY GOD?

Are you pursuing whatever you're currently pursuing because you're so darn good at it, or because one day God encountered you and said, "I want to use you in this way." And something in your heart said, "Yes Lord, I am willing. Send me!" Then, maybe along the way you started to get it into your head, "Well now I need to get prepared. I need to get qualified. I need to prove that I am ready to do the thing God called me to do and that He made a good choice in picking me!" Yes, you need to prepare. I'm a firm believer in seminary, education, training, apprenticeship and degrees. But never, never let yourself begin to believe that what equips you to do what you are doing is also what qualifies you. It's God's calling on your life that qualifies you; the One who prepared you from long ago to do good things.

My hope for you is that when you look at your role and your leadership, wherever it may be, that you'll say with confidence, "God, you have called me, and that is enough."

CHAPTER 8
STAYING SAFE

What a journey we've been on together! We've seen how a culture of grace begins with me. As I let God see all of my stuff and receive His relentless love, I am transformed to be a grace-giver. We've seen how hiding, ignoring, and justifying sin never leads to real freedom. Only the forgiveness Jesus offers as we face truth leads us to our best day. We've seen how shame causes us to hide and believe we have to cover our brokenness; but God's truth calls us out to see ourselves as God does—His unique creation. We've seen how confession to God and others, painful as it may be, opens the door to true intimacy and community. We've recognized how grace brings us from forgotten "pasture-less" places and seats us at God's family table. We've understood the freedom to live out of the grace of God's calling and not the pressure of our performance. All of these are attitudes of the heart that will keep us on a path of grace.

Yet this path, like so many others, must be attended to carefully or we can easily find ourselves off course. The lure of legalism will attempt to pull us back to simplistic black and white thinking. The whisper of postmodern thinking will tempt us to abandon truth. But one voice may pull more people off the path of grace than any other: the cheap substitute of acceptance. We'll deal with that concept as we enter our last leg of the journey together.

YEAH, BUT...

Over the last several years, I have watched our society become an increasingly divided place. Have you? We argue over immigration and refugees. We debate about climate change and regulating the pollution level from big companies. We fight about the rights of unborn babies over or against the rights of pregnant mothers. We point fingers at the Lesbian, Gay, Bisexual, Transgender and Queer (LGBTQ) community, or at those who judge and dehumanize them.

I'm not in anyway sparking a political debate or attempting to weigh in on *any* of these hot-button, important debates. What I am guessing is that somewhere in that list, your heart quickened as you read. You found yourself personally engaged, and emotional, about one or more of those topics. Like never before, we have attached the issues of our day to the emotions of our heart. We easily feel separated from those who disagree with us. In the chasm that opens between us, people today clamor for acceptance.

I wonder if this scenario—this climate of disagreement echoing all around us—has led us to a tragic misunderstanding of grace. "Grace," for many, has become a generic word, used on both sides of any argument, to explain what a kind-hearted person ought to have for someone who disagrees with them. When we choose to overlook someone's error in thinking or judgment, and treat them as a human-being instead, this is thought of as grace.

Grace becomes a catch-all word that says, "I choose to accept you for who you are even though I disagree with you."

CHAPTER 8: STAYING SAFE

This idea may describe a culture of acceptance. This could even be called a culture of love. Our culture could certainly use more acceptance and more love!

But this is not a culture of grace. Let me explain.

GRACE STORIES

Think about this: Every great story of grace in Scripture involves someone coming in fear and humility, believing they deserved some retribution for their actions. They have broken the bonds of a covenant relationship, and they know it. They know they are worthy of rejection, hatred or punishment. So when they receive forgiveness instead, this becomes a story of grace.

Consider these short summaries of stories from the Bible:

Jacob deceives his brother, Esau, and his father, in order to steal the birthright of the first-born son. Fearing his brother's retribution, he flees to a far-off land where he works long enough to marry both Rebekah and Leah, and amass a great wealth. At last, when he returns to his family home, he sends every gift imaginable to his brother to pacify his anger. At their meeting, Esau chooses to embrace him. Grace.

Joseph's brothers throw him in a pit for dead; then, in pity, sell him as a slave to Egypt. Many years later, the roles are completely reversed as Joseph stands unrecognized as the second-in-command of Egypt and the brothers are begging him for food. Rather than revenge, which would have been expected in his Egyptian culture, he chooses compassion, and all Israel survives. Grace.

Yet again, when Joseph's father dies, the 11 brothers slink back to Joseph fearful they will get their due from Joseph, now that their father is gone. Instead, Joseph proclaims to them, "You intended to harm me, but God intended it for good to accomplish what is now being done, the saving of many lives. So then, don't be afraid."[69] The brothers come in humility. Joseph has the power to condemn. Grace is given.

God instructs the prophet Hosea to marry the prostitute Gomer as an example of how God has remained loving toward Israel, even though the country has been faithless. Hosea obeys, they have children together, and then Gomer runs off again. That's it, end of story, right? Hosea has done what God asked. But then God commands Hosea to go and redeem her again. He buys her out of slavery and covers over her ignominy. Not only does Gomer receive grace, but the story illustrates God's incredible grace for Israel—though the country deserves judgment, God will again lavish love on them if they will turn back to Him.

As we looked at earlier, the prodigal son returns home, believing his actions make him worthy of nothing more than serving as a hired hand. He has disrespected, and disowned, the father, not to mention wasting a significant chunk of his wealth. But the father has been waiting for him, and rushes to lavish on the son all the good gifts he can bestow. The son deserves nothing and knows it. The father also knows, but chooses to give freely of his riches. Grace is poured out on one who knows he doesn't deserve it.

In every one of these stories, can you see the common equation? First, an act—or long series of actions—leads a person away from relationship. Second, some shift is made, either willingly or out of necessity, that forces the person back to the relationship they

---

69. Genesis 50:20

CHAPTER 8: STAYING SAFE

have broken. Third, the person to whom they return has the power, and even the right, to punish or condemn them. In each story, the one returning *knows* this would be a just outcome for their behavior. But finally, instead of the merited punishment, the person in the position of power offers forgiveness, and the gift of a restored relationship. This is grace at work.

How does this differ from the kind of grace many people seem to want today? The kind of grace expected in many instances is a grace without step three. Rather than acknowledging any wrong has been done, or believing any condemnation is deserved, they simply believe unmerited favor should be theirs.

You could almost say that some feel entitled to grace. Grace and entitlement never go together. Without the humility produced by an awareness of our hurtful action or sinful steps, the grace given is merely permission. Rather than, "Go and sin no more"[70] the message is, "Go and continue doing what you've been doing." This will never lead to change.

Grace cost Jesus too much for Him to give us that kind of cheap grace.

Consider those who missed grace in Scripture. Notice in these stories how they believed they had nothing to repent of:

Cain kills his brother, Abel, and when confronted by God, sidesteps the whole conversation, "Who am I? My brother's keeper?" Grace was not given. Cain is sent from the garden under a curse.

Unrepentant Israel is given over to her enemies time and time again in the Old Testament. At every opportunity the Lord cries out, "Turn from your wicked ways!" Yet Israel continues blindly in her idolatry. Grace is absent.

---

70. John 8:11

The Pharisees, who travel over land and sea to make a single convert, would not stoop down to help someone in need near them. The Pharisees excused their lack of compassion by a cloak of knowledge and religiosity. They not only missed Jesus, but they missed grace as well. It is to them that Jesus says, "It is not the healthy who need a doctor, but the sick!"[71]

Ananias and Sapphira try to cheat the church, and God, out of some money while still looking spiritual and generous. The apostle Peter gives each, in turn, a chance to own their sin. When they persist in their charade, the Holy Spirit strikes them dead.[72] Where was grace? Unavailable to two people who were convinced they didn't need it.

In each story, those who thought they could abuse God or His covenant because of grace ended up missing out on both God and His grace.

THE HONEST TRUTH

There will be some who come to us and plead for or, more likely, demand grace. They like the idea of Jesus, and they love the idea of love; but they don't want to own their stuff, acknowledge their sin, or practice any sort of humility.

So the warning is this: Grace offered to an unrepentant heart will never be received as grace. An unrepentant heart doesn't truly want grace, but license. Give me my freedom to live in the way that I want. We can choose this, but it isn't grace.

---

71. Matthew 9:12
72. Acts 5:1-11

CHAPTER 8: STAYING SAFE

Grace may help to eventually soften their hardness of heart, but more often than not it will be rejected. I cannot think of a single example in Scripture where grace was effectively received by someone who was closed off to their own need for it. All the great stories of sin and grace—David and Bathsheba, the woman caught in adultery, the prodigal son—spring from the repentant turning of a rebellious heart. Many other stories—those of the Pharisees, or Absalom, or Ananias and Sapphira—don't include grace because it couldn't be received. No repentance. No turning. Only entitlement.

As we looked at earlier, grace isn't found in the absence of sin, but the abundance of it. Paul, at the end of his life, calls himself the "Chief of Sinners."[73] I can think of much better things I'd like to be the chief of, but here is Paul, after 25 years of planting the church and writing the Bible, declaring himself the worst of sinners. Was he sinning more? No, but he was more aware of his sin, so he was receiving more grace. Look at his letters and you'll see how much he loved grace! He can't get more than a few verses, it seems, without declaring the wonders of God's grace for all who come broken to Him.

At times, to be a safe place and safe people, it may mean that we stand against those who would abuse the culture of grace. We can do so lovingly. We can speak the truth in love. But we need to be firm enough to say that grace and entitlement can't co-exist.

I remember one time walking through a particularly challenging situation in our church family where a man in a troubled marriage kept appealing to our "grace." He wanted us to give him the grace we were becoming well-known for. Looking

---

73. I Timothy 1:16

back, I believe we were gracious! We were helping him get a place to live, to breathe and think clearly, providing him with counseling, and asking for some significant changes from his wife.

But when we continued to point out that he was pursuing a divorce based on his own desire for happiness, spurning the advice of his friends and church, he walked away. How could we be so "grace-less" to suggest he own his sin? His accusation was that we didn't love him enough to just agree with his actions. The truth was, we loved him so much! As hard as it was, we recognized that only in embracing the pain of his sinfulness could he ever discover the wonder of true grace. We spoke the truth in love, but in the end real grace was rejected in favor of personal comfort.

Grace isn't some weak, willy-nilly acceptance of any and all behavior under the sun. Grace is loving people enough to humbly invite them to participate with God in being transformed.

If someone is demanding grace from you without any humility on their part, or recognition of sin, or willingness to change, you can love them, but grace won't help. Instead, you may need to set some boundaries, speak the truth in love, and be willing to let them walk away. Those topics are tough, multi-layered, and the subject of many other books.

If they do walk away, be willing to wait like the father of the prodigal, looking eagerly for their return. We don't write them off or turn off our heart. We hope and pray for the day when an encounter of real grace will come. We await the turning of their heart.

PATH CHOSEN

Recently, my family and I moved to within a few miles of the mouth of the Columbia River Gorge. This area is known for strong

CHAPTER 8: STAYING SAFE

winds, big truck stops, and gorgeous landscapes. The wide valley cut by the Columbia River has created a series of breathtaking waterfalls and some of the best hiking I've ever found. We are very excited to be just a few minutes away from one of the best recreational areas the west has to offer.

One summer, I took my four kids on an adventure—a hike above the Multnomah Falls area. We spent a fun afternoon splashing around in the stream and enjoying a picnic lunch. At the end of our adventure, we made our way back down to the base of the falls, where they have a fantastic visitor's center (and some of the largest chocolate chip cookies I have ever seen in my life).

Inside the visitor's center is a large, contoured map of the whole falls area: a series of dozens of waterfalls. We stood over that map for quite some time, mouths full of chocolate chip cookie, tracing with our fingers where all the various paths led. Some paths connected to one another, some looped back on themselves, and some led to the peaks of mountains. On this series of trails, you will find many, many forks in the path. Choose the one on the right, and you may find yourself tackling a 2,000 foot ascent. Choose the path to the left, and you may end up at a parking lot, some miles from where you left your car.

The path you choose to walk on makes all the difference in the destination you'll reach. So it is with grace.

In the first chapter of this book, I reviewed many of the wrong paths we may have taken along the way that perpetuate a climate of shame and prevent us from being a culture of grace. As we close this book, let's look back at these and see what truths we have picked up along the way that contradict the errant trails.

WRONG PATH 1: WE REACT TO SIN AND CONFESSION WITH SHOCK, SURPRISE, OR AN ATTITUDE OF SUPERIORITY.

Truth 1: Celebrate openness, confession, and humility by ushering people into safe communities for change and restoration. Once we get in touch, and stay in touch, with the fallenness of our own heart, our reaction to the fallenness of others will change. Rather than reacting in a judgmental or hyper-religious way, we respond with empathy and an invitation to true community. The words that spring from our lips become, "I'm so proud of you for sharing." "I've been where you are." "Thanks for your honesty—it's a huge step in the right direction." When our community becomes marked by this type of response to sin, we will find that we have many more willing sinners in our midst! Willing—not by their behavior or desire to sin more—but willing to be open and real about what is already there.

WRONG PATH 2: WE BELIEVE THAT CHANGE IS SIMPLE.

Truth 2: Create a small group structure that will walk with people for the long-haul of change. Grace teaches us that change is painful and an often costly process. We have watched in our own lives the way we must grit our teeth and fight for every inch of forward progress away from the selfishness of our souls. We recognize the way our brain has been trained in one direction, and rewiring these information superhighways takes time and intentionality. When we embrace that change is most often a long and slow process, we can commit to people for the long-haul. We evaluate progress, not by the speed of the change, but by the consistency of effort being made in the same direction.

CHAPTER 8: STAYING SAFE

WRONG PATH 3: CHURCH DISCIPLINE THAT EMPHASIZES PUNISHMENT INSTEAD OF RESTORATION.

Truth 3: Center church discipline around relationship and healthy mentorship. A culture of grace is always about leading people back into community. For the person walking through discipline, this emphasis makes it safe to stay. Seemingly, we all possess a side of us that assumes: if they pay for what they've done, they'll learn their lesson. In a culture of grace, we see that punishment without community only creates rejection and shame. The goal of discipline is ALWAYS a more loved (and mature) disciple.

WRONG PATH 4: CREATING A CULTURE WHERE CERTAIN TOPICS ARE TABOO.

Truth 4: We humbly and openly talk about everything in our preaching and teaching (in culturally-appropriate and age-appropriate ways). Grace is focused on the restoration of the heart, not righting every wrong. What this means is that we accept that every heart, apart from Christ, is twisted and wicked. We cease to be surprised at any level of evil emerging from the center of the old self. Rather than fixating on the behavior to be corrected, we look to redeeming the heart by reuniting it with the Creator and the people who walk in the Creator's redemption. If this is the case, then no topic feels off limits or taboo. Every sin, every behavior, every addiction becomes an opportunity to see God do a marvelous work.

WRONG PATH 5: ONLY TELLING THE HAPPY STORIES.

Truth 5: Regularly use testimonies of people who are "in process," but discovering a new measure of freedom and transformation. In grace, we accept that not every story is happy; or at least we accept that not every part of every story is happy. We always hope for one to emerge, but along the way most stories are filled with trial, struggle and pain. Yet how many times have we seen that these places of difficulty are the very same realm where God and His grace are most readily seen? If we only tell the happy stories, we miss telling the moments that will most readily connect with our audience. More often than not, people relate to our pain, not our victory. And when we tell of meeting Jesus in our pain, we offer that same grace to a multitude of others. At least once a quarter, have someone share a story of how God is redeeming and using their messy situation.

WRONG PATH 6: HONORING THE FINISHED PRODUCT AND NOT THE PROCESS.

Truth 6: Model vulnerability and growth in your leadership. When you start to walk in grace, you begin to see that most of the "finished products" out there are mainly a facade covering the unaddressed fissures of the soul. This side of heaven, we won't meet many finished products. But we will meet countless people who need to know that wherever they are in their process is a place where Jesus can meet them. When we celebrate the various stages of the journey toward maturity, we give people freedom to be present in that stage. Honoring the process honors the God who leads us through the process of change.

CHAPTER 8: STAYING SAFE

WRONG PATH 7: REPLICATING THE DYSFUNCTION OF THE HOME.

Truth 7: Face the dysfunction of the home and allow God to "re-parent" us! Grace gives us permission to accept that our families, no matter how good or godly, were not perfect. From this place of honest assessment, we can see where God needs to redeem our pattern of family interaction. Then, rather than replicating the kind of parenting we received in other contexts, we are able to "re-parent" one another in the Fatherhood of God. We make Him our model for every kind of relationship and His word the standard for family interaction. Whether the subject is conflict, forgiveness, or discipline, we seek to replicate His pattern of family.

WRONG PATH 8: A VIEW THAT TRANSFORMATION IS KNOWLEDGE-BASED.

Truth 8: Emphasize the loving relationships we all need in order to be healed. Knowledge, when practiced alone, puffs up. Love builds up. Love has a way of addressing our deepest questions of value and belonging. When we cement the rule of Christ's love in our hearts, we begin to believe we are people worthy of love. His love always precedes our change. How does that kind of love work its way into us? Through others. When we love as Christ loved us, we invite one another into real transformation.

STANDING IN HIS HOLY PLACE

Just like being lost on a hike through the mountains, identifying the wrong trail and getting off of it is only half the battle. The right path must still be traveled. Stretching before us, inviting as it may be, is a rigorous path called grace. We are invited on a daunting adventure of becoming a safe place and safe people. The journey isn't always easy: it takes painful honesty, requires we rub shoulders with other broken people, and, at times, seems to demand more of us than we have to give. We may even be tempted to turn downhill and walk on easier paths of judgment, isolation or religious superiority.

But only one path takes us closer to His throne. As the Psalmist proclaims:

> *Who may ascend the mountain of the LORD?*
> *Who may stand in his holy place?*
> *The one who has clean hands and a pure heart,*
> *Who does not trust in an idol...*[74]

As you read that verse, you may find yourself wondering what it has to do with grace. With all due respect to the authors of the New International Version, I wonder if they didn't miss the mark at the end of verse 4. The Hebrew word for "idol" here is most commonly translated as falsehood (SHAV)—a word for vanity and deception. The worship of false idols is condemned throughout Scripture, but I don't think this was David's intent in Psalm 24. He is answering the question, "Who can stand in the presence of God?" And his answer is to declare, "The One in whom there is nothing pretended, put on, or false." Or, as the New American Standard Bible reads, *"(he) who has not lifted up his soul to falsehood..."*

Think about this visual picture for a moment: How did someone attain clean hands, in the Old Testament times, or now? Simply put, by washing them. Washing hands implies they were dirty and needed a good scrubbing. Too often, when we read about

---

74. Psalm 24:3, 4 NIV

CHAPTER 8: STAYING SAFE

clean hands in Scripture we think of someone who has no sin or "filth" in their life. At least I do. Here, the idea David celebrates is of those who have cleansed themselves, *because their hands were dirty*! Having washed their hands—through confession and facing truth—they continue to walk in a place of truth, refusing to live in any falsehood or vanity.

In other words, what qualifies people for the journey up the mountain of the Lord is that their hands were dirty, and then washed clean. They didn't show up with clean hands. So, we can continue our journey with confidence; knowing God is safe to approach with dirty hands.

That, my friends, is a path of grace. In the wonderful, all-encompassing grace of the Father, we allow Him to wash our hands, and our lives, of all the filth we've gotten ourselves into. Then, we look down at our clean hands as a sign of His love and acceptance of us. In this place, we long to stay there—to stay real and honest before Him. We refuse to put on falsehood or to try and lift up a pretend version of ourselves. Instead, we lift up our true-self for Him to love.

Do you want to walk with God? The path involves clean hands (forgiveness) and a commitment to walk in the truth of who we are as people with cleansed hands (grace). Those who walk in grace, walk with God. As the thoughts in Psalm 24 concludes:

> *They will receive the LORD's blessing and have a right relationship with God their savior.*[75]

May we be among those who walk in grace and may we trace the path for others to follow in our steps.

---

75. Psalm 24:5